# PREPPER'S LONG-TERM SURVIVAL GUIDE

ALL YOU NEED TO KNOW TO SURVIVE EVERYWHERE DURING A DISASTER BE PREPARED IN CASE OF EMERGENCY AND PROTECT YOUR FAMILY WITHOUT WAITING FOR THE RESCUE

MARK SUNDERLAND

© **Copyright 2022 - Mark Sunderland. All rights reserved.**

The content contained within this book may not be reproduced , duplicated or transmitted without direct written permission from the author or the publisher.
Under no circumstances will any blame or legal responsibility be heald against the publisher, or author, for any damages, reparation, or monetary loss due to the information contained within this book. Either directly or indirectly.

**Legal notice:**

This book is copyright protected. This book is only for personal use. You cannot amend, distribute, sell, use, quote or paraphrase any part, or the content within this book, without the consent of the author or publisher.

**Disclaimer Notice:**

Please note the information contained within this document is for educational and entertainment purposes only. All effort has been executed to present accurate, up-to-date, and reliable, complete information, No warranties of any kind are declared or implied. Readers acknowledge that the author is not engaging in the rendering of legal, financial, medical, or professional advice. The content within this book has been derived from various sources. Please consult a licensed professional before attempting any techniques outlined in this book.

By reading this document, the reader agrees that under no circumstances is the author responsible for any loss, direct or indirect, which is incurred as a result of the use of the information contained within this document, including, but not limited to, errors, omissions, or inaccuracies

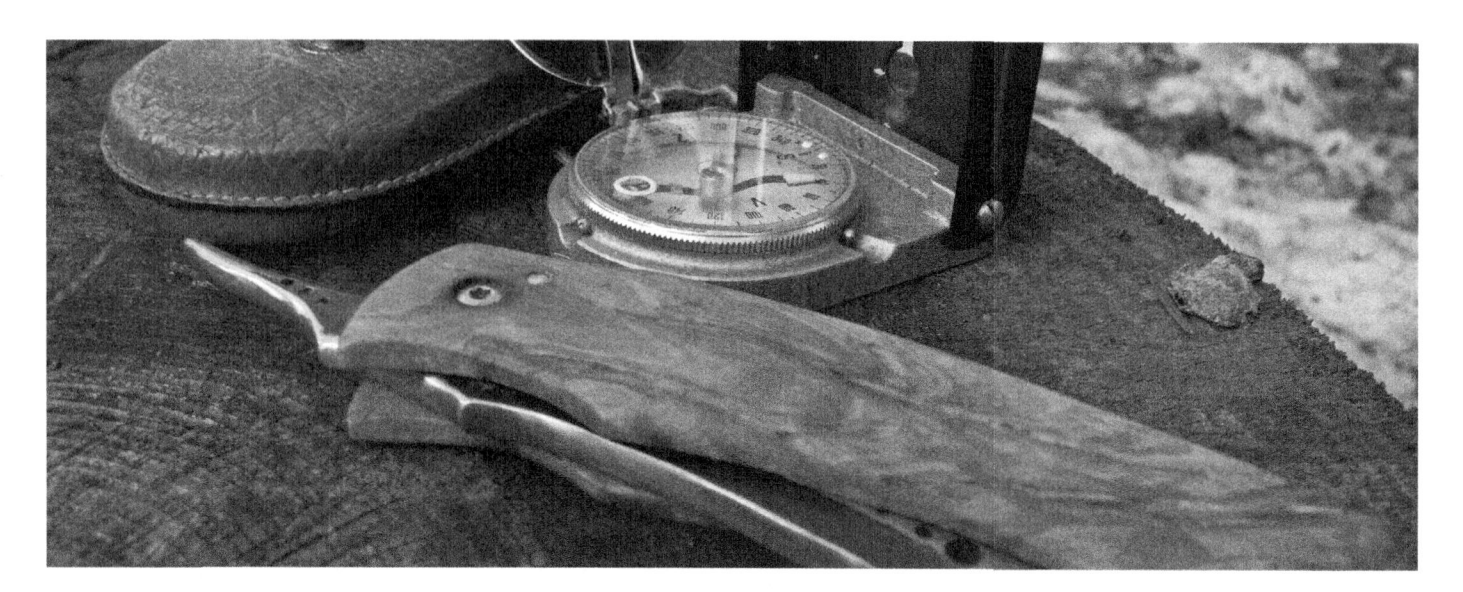

# TABLE OF CONTENT

## BOOK 1: ........................................................... 8
## PREPPING FUNDAMENTALS ........................ 8

### CHAPTER 1: WHY DO WE PREPPING? ........ 9

| | |
|---|---|
| Leadership Qualities | 9 |
| Acquire Responsibility | 9 |
| Improved Health | 9 |
| Improved Relationships | 9 |
| Loss of Employment | 9 |
| You'll Be Less Stressed | 9 |
| New Interests | 9 |
| You Might Be Able to Save a Life | 9 |
| Pandemics | 9 |
| You'll Be Less Bored and Lonely | 10 |
| You Discover Appreciation | 10 |
| Car Trouble | 10 |
| Nature Rediscovered | 10 |
| Financial Failure | 10 |
| You Develop Self-Sufficiency | 10 |
| You Might Make Money | 11 |
| Negotiation Training | 11 |
| Creating a Long-term Food Supply | 11 |
| Spend Less Money | 11 |

### CHAPTER 2: PREPPER'S MINDSET ............ 11

| | |
|---|---|
| Preparation Mentality | 11 |
| Mental Health Survival Guide | 12 |
| Preppers' Equipment's Checklist | 13 |
| Important Documents | 14 |
| How to Prepare Your Family for Strenuous Situations | 15 |
| Survival Skills for Children and the Elderly | 16 |
| Developing Children's Emergency Preparedness | 17 |

## BOOK 2: ........................................................... 18
## BUG-IN: YOUR HOME IS YOUR GREATEST SURVIVAL SHELTER ............ 18

### YOUR HOME IS YOUR GREATEST SURVIVAL SHELTER ............ 19

| | |
|---|---|
| Checklist for Bugging-in Essentials | 19 |
| Likely Bug-in Scenarios | 19 |
| Self Defense | 20 |

## BOOK 3: ........................................................... 22
## FOOD ............................................................... 22

### CHAPTER 1: HOW TO ORGANIZE YOUR PANTRY AND SUPPLIES – THE PREPPER'S PANTRY ............ 23

| | |
|---|---|
| Necessary Equipment and Tools for Food Storage | 23 |
| Prepping the Pantry | 24 |
| Keep the Food Fresh | 24 |
| Tracking the Pantry | 24 |
| Essential Foods to Have Inside the Pantry | 25 |
| How Long Can You Store Food? | 28 |
| How to Organize Your Pantry? | 29 |
| Additional Food Pantry Organization Tips | 31 |

### CHAPTER 2: LONG-TERM FOOD STORAGE METHODS ............ 31

| | |
|---|---|
| Short-Term Storage of Food | 32 |
| Long-Term Storage of Food | 33 |
| The Rotation of Long-Term Storage Food alongside the Short-Term Storage Food | 33 |
| Fermentation | 34 |
| Dehydrating | 34 |
| Canning | 36 |
| Freezing | 38 |
| Other Food Preservation Techniques | 38 |

### CHAPTER 3: TYPES OF CEREALS FOR STORAGE ............ 39

# PREPPER'S LONG-TERM SURVIVAL GUIDE

| | |
|---|---|
| Delicate Grains | 39 |
| Hard Grains | 40 |
| Dry Pasta | 40 |
| Flour | 40 |
| Beans | 40 |

## CHAPTER 4: THE ART OF GETTING BY — 40

| | |
|---|---|
| A Guide to Identifying, Collecting and Preparing Wild Edible Plants | 40 |
| Growing Your Own Food Is an Environmentally Sustainable Way to Produce Food | 42 |
| Raising Animals | 42 |
| Fishing, Hunting, and Trapping | 47 |
| Cooking Off-the-Grid | 50 |

# BOOK 4:
# WATER — 55

## CHAPTER 1: THE IMPORTANCE OF WATER — 56

| | |
|---|---|
| Water Purification Techniques | 57 |
| The Risks of Drinking Unpurified Water | 61 |

## CHAPTER 2: HOW TO STORE IT? — 61

| | |
|---|---|
| Water Storage and Handling | 62 |
| Why Keep Water for Such a Long Time? | 63 |
| How to Store Water in a Survival Situation | 63 |
| How Much Water Should You Store? | 64 |
| Water Storage Containers | 64 |
| Making Water Plan | 65 |
| How to Make a Water Containment System | 66 |
| Testing Well Water | 67 |
| Water Sources in and around Your Home | 67 |

## CHAPTER 3: YOU'LL NEVER RUN OUT OF WATER: RENEWABLE WATER SOURCES — 68

| | |
|---|---|
| Finding a Safe Water Source in the Wilderness | 69 |
| Rainwater | 69 |
| Rivers, Streams, or Lakes | 70 |
| Creeks and Ponds | 71 |
| Collecting Groundwater | 71 |
| Finding Hidden Sources of Water | 71 |

# BOOK 5:
# HYGIENE — 73

| | |
|---|---|
| Supplies | 74 |
| Personal Cleanliness | 76 |
| Washing Your Hands, the Right Way | 76 |
| Oral Hygiene and Health | 76 |
| Feminine Hygiene | 77 |
| Wounds and Injuries Cleaning | 77 |
| Taking Care of Babies When Living Off-Grid | 77 |
| Toilet Facilities | 77 |
| Laundry | 78 |
| Waste Disposal | 79 |
| Keeping Warm | 79 |
| Clothing | 80 |

# BOOK 6:
# ENERGY — 82

## ARE YOU READY FOR A BLACKOUT? — 83

| | |
|---|---|
| The Blackout Survival Kit | 83 |
| Recommended Power Sources | 83 |
| How to Cook without Power | 88 |
| Lighting Fire | 89 |
| Alternate Light Sources | 89 |

# BOOK 7:
# SECURITY — 91

## KEEPING SAFE — 92

| | |
|---|---|
| Security Lighting and Alarms | 92 |
| Watch Dogs | 93 |
| Protect Your Garage | 95 |
| Use Locks Everywhere in Your House | 95 |
| Hiding Places | 96 |

## TABLE OF CONTENT

| | |
|---|---|
| Use Warning Signs | 96 |
| Perimeter Defense | 97 |
| Early Warning Systems | 97 |
| Traps and Funneling | 97 |
| Windows Security Is a Must-Have | 98 |
| Walls Provide Protection | 99 |
| Nighttime Security | 99 |
| Fire Safety | 99 |
| Defensive Weapons | 100 |
| Situational Awareness | 101 |
| Landscape | 102 |
| | 102 |

# BOOK 8: 103

# HEALTH 103

## CHAPTER 1: THE PREPPER'S INFIRMARY 104

| | |
|---|---|
| Medical Emergency Survival Guide | 105 |
| Survival First-Aid Kit | 107 |
| First-Aid Tips in Different Emergency Situations | 108 |
| Survival Medicine Guide | 113 |
| Using an Emergency Plan Template | 114 |
| Keeping Your First-Aid Kit Current | 115 |

## CHAPTER 2: NATURAL REMEDIES 116

Know Your Herb 116

How to Create a Home Medicine Cabinet Using Natural Remedies 120

# BOOK 9: 122

# BUG OUT 122

## WHEN YOUR HOME IS NO LONGER SAFE 123

| | |
|---|---|
| When should one Decide to Bug Out? | 123 |
| Bug-Out Checklist | 123 |
| How to Make a Bug-Out Bag? | 124 |
| How to Find a New Shelter | 127 |
| Types of Outdoor Shelters | 128 |

| | |
|---|---|
| Shelter Characteristics | 130 |
| How to Make a Shelter Safe | 133 |
| Communication Strategy | 135 |
| Land Navigation Techniques | 138 |

# BOOK 10: 143

# THE MOST FREQUENT SHTF SITUATIONS: TIPS AND TRICKS 143

| | |
|---|---|
| THE MOST FREQUENT SHTF SITUATIONS: TIPS AND TRICKS | 144 |
| Bug Out Situations That Are Most Likely to Occur | 144 |

# CONCLUSION 149

# REFERENCES 150

# INTRODUCTION

The world in which we live is unpredictable. It's full of dangers that can appear at any time. This guide will provide you with valuable information that will enable you to deal with these situations appropriately when they arise. My book provides simple instructions and procedures that can be used by people of all backgrounds and skill levels, young and old alike.

A lot of things can happen that cause chaos and turmoil. It is best to be prepared with all necessary items to increase their chances of survival if such misfortunes occur.

Everyone will be confronted with an emergency at some point in their lives. An earthquake, another natural disaster, a pandemic, or even war are all possibilities. If life has taught us anything, it is to always be prepared for the worst.

If you're not sure where to begin preparing for a disaster or emergency, this book will guide you through the process. You will be guided through the entire process, beginning with mentally and emotionally preparing yourself.

Preparing for the worst is simply to assist you if something terrible occurs in your life and to aid in your recovery from these events. The best part about preparing for the worst is making sure you're doing it correctly, have the right information, and that those around you are doing the same.

You must understand the fundamentals of prepping and ask yourself why you need to prepare for any situation. Modern-day preppers are attempting to prepare for a specific time when life becomes difficult. They intend to be self-sufficient and independent enough to face any challenge, no matter how difficult. You'll find that you have most of what you need with a little diligence and planning.

To be more specific, a prepper is someone who has expert wisdom and thoughtful insight into the future. And this ideology and logical thinking assist them in preparing for all possible events that may occur in their lives. Prepping is all about taking reasonable steps to prepare for a better future for everyone. It intends to assist them in making better use of their time so that they can enjoy the present.

Prepping is the process by which preppers adapt to be capable of dealing with almost anything that violates the peace around them. It is the approach that promotes anticipating and planning for potential risk factors and the necessary needs to overcome them.

# PREPPING FUNDAMENTALS

Prepping is the process of preparing for survival without the use of complex infrastructure. It is the action that promotes being ready to face life before, during, and after an apocalyptic event.

If you want to understand what this concept offers to the modern world, you should be familiar with more detailed concepts and descriptions about preppers and prepping.

Another issue that comes with disasters is that you may have to survive without any technology or electricity, and you can meet these unforeseen events by having a handy survival kit and being well prepared. It will also lessen your reliance on emergency services.

Another advantage of prepping is that you will have to live without modern conveniences on which we humans are inherently dependent. We have become overly reliant on technology and power in recent years. We also take them for granted, assuming that there will never be a time when we will need them. Thus, prepping will assist us in overcoming such dependency and difficulties when a disaster strikes.

Preparing is neither difficult nor expensive. All it takes is practice and a clear mind. It also necessitates organizational control and coordination skills. Though it may appear new and modern to some, prepping is not a new practice. Preppers believe in self-sufficiency and accept responsibility for their own safety and security.

You must maintain hope and believe that you can survive. You must remove any unnecessary material attachments to keep yourself and your family safe. You will have to leave several expensive or sentimental items behind, but these should be the least of your concerns. Maintain a healthy level of physical activity and remember to consume adequate nutrients and vitamins at all times. You must also be adaptable and quick. Aside from physical strength, you will also need to sort things out, which will require energy.

Having the right mindset is one of the most difficult aspects of dealing with a crisis. It will be much easier to deal with this process if you understand that there are basic steps that must be taken and have an idea of what needs to be done. You may not know where to begin or what to do, but having a plan in mind will help you figure out the specific steps.

Mental discipline and conditioning will aid your survival by allowing you to maintain your cool under pressure. That way, you will be able to make rational decisions that will assist you in staying focused and making sound decisions.

With a survival book like this, you will be able to react confidently in certain situations while also gaining the necessary technical knowledge. You will also understand what kind of items, medicine, and equipment you can use to ensure that you are always one step ahead of the mishap at hand.

You will become mentally stronger, more resourceful, and better prepared for potentially hazardous situations if you incorporate these tips and basic skills. Soon, you will discover that much of what you learn here will find its way into your daily life and will do so in unexpected ways. Get in the habit of saying, "I'm glad I was prepared for that!"

This knowledge has been proven time and again through countless experiences. Some of this wisdom, however simple, has held for thousands of years. Other sections will make use of modern advancements.

Let's get started.

# BOOK 1: PREPPING FUNDAMENTALS

# PREPPING FUNDAMENTALS

## CHAPTER 1: WHY DO WE PREPPING?

**Leadership Qualities**

You must become a leader if you want to lead your family to survival. You must have a vision, learn to encourage others, resolve conflicts, and be the necessary leader. You must, however, learn how to lead without coming across as overly critical and bossy!

**Acquire Responsibility**

Becoming a prepper entails taking responsibility for yourself as well as those in your prepper family.

**Improved Health**

Drills, hikes, and eating better, organic food all lead to a healthier you—getting in shape now means being prepared for when the SHTF. You'll eat less junk food and more vitamins, minerals, and macronutrients to help your body stay healthy.

**Improved Relationships**

You have no choice—planning for the end of the world requires teamwork, and prepping can bring even the most estranged families back together. Hiking, camping, and even watching survival shows on TV can all help.

**Loss of Employment**

Losing a job is one of the most terrifying domestic events. Not only is losing a job disruptive, but it can also lead to bankruptcy and homelessness. You're already ahead of the game if you've started stockpiling food, emergency funds and working toward self-sufficiency. However, now is the time to prepare for job loss. After that, there are several steps you can take to improve your chances of survival.

**You'll Be Less Stressed**

Rather than complaining about what the world is becoming, spend your time preparing. There will be less weight on your shoulders, and you will be able to go through life feeling happier, knowing that you are prepared for whatever happens.

**New Interests**

Camping, hiking, fishing, learning to build fires, finding water sources—the list goes on and on. Grow your own food, learn new cooking skills, do woodwork, DIY, and so on.

**You Might Be Able to Save a Life**

Learning basic first aid and survival medicine is always useful, and you might be able to use your skills to save a life one day when no other help is available.

**Pandemics**

Many people wonder how they can prepare for a COVID-19 pandemic as the novel coronavirus spreads worldwide. Many of the supplies in a well-stocked preparedness kit are useful even if the

# PREPPER'S LONG-TERM SURVIVAL GUIDE

virus is not as severe as recent ones. Basic supplies should always be on hand, and public health officials will issue additional instructions as needed.

Every hospital should be equipped to care for COVID-19 patients while also providing other critical medical services to their communities. However, as the pandemic progresses, the definition of "appropriate care" will shift, so hospitals and healthcare providers should work together to develop contingency plans. CDC Flu Surge projections can assist healthcare providers and businesses in making appropriate plans. Hospital CEOs should discuss these concerns with their boards of directors and how to allocate limited resources and training.

**You'll Be Less Bored and Lonely**

Many people are bored and see no one. Prepping changes all of that; not only will your new skills keep you busy, but you can also join a preppers group and meet new people.

**You Discover Appreciation**

Everyone is guilty of overlooking the significance of the little things—a bottle of water, an apple from your tree, or finishing that ten-mile hike. Count your lucky stars!

**Car Trouble**

You'll have a vehicle that won't break down if you're prepared for survival. Even though cars are much more reliable these days, they can still fail. There are, thankfully, ways to prepare for a car breakdown, one of which is to plan for roadside assistance. Prepare yourself by stocking your car's emergency roadside kit with tools and spare parts if your vehicle is old or in poor condition. Additional tools can also be purchased from a local hardware store.

Staying near a gas station is a good way to prepare for a car breakdown. Check that you're close enough to cell phone coverage to call a friend for help. If you find yourself in the middle of nowhere, keep bottled water on hand. You should also bring a survival lighter with you. Matches, which are the most dependable survival lighters, can also be carried.

**Nature Rediscovered**

Do you spend your days alternating between the office and your living room couch? Hiking and camping get you outside in nature, which has many benefits for you and your life.

**Financial Failure**

One of the first things to do if you are in a position to prepare for a financial collapse is to save a large amount of emergency savings. Ideally, you should keep these funds in a checking account where you can easily access them. Avoid term deposit accounts that have withdrawal limits if at all possible. It's also a good idea to keep some cash on hand as an emergency reserve. You'll need to stretch this money as far as possible, so get rid of any unnecessary debt.

**You Develop Self-Sufficiency**

Dependence on others is all too common in today's society, and while it won't be possible to go completely off-grid, you can learn self-reliance in a variety of ways—how far you take it is entirely up to you.

# PREPPING FUNDAMENTALS

**You Might Make Money**

Selling surplus crops to neighbors or at the market (using your survival skills) teaches you to help others while earning an income, and you can even teach others how to survive. Simply be aware of the tax laws that apply to earning extra money and the requirements for handling food.

**Negotiation Training**

As a prepper, you learn to barter, which is a form of negotiation. Begin bartering right away to hone your skills.

Now that you know why you should start prepping keep reading to find out what else you should know.

**Creating a Long-term Food Supply**

We must reduce our meat consumption and increase our plant-based diet for the sake of sustainability. A plant-based diet has numerous health benefits and is an excellent way to reduce our environmental footprint. Furthermore, we should avoid eating processed foods and meat. Eating a sustainable diet can avoid many of the problems associated with meat. There are, however, ways to make our diet more sustainable. In this case, you should try to eat a flexitarian diet, which is mostly plant-based but includes some meat and fish.

**Spend Less Money**

Survival doesn't need to cost a fortune; there are loads of things you can do right now to save money, including:

- Growing your own food.
- Making your home safer without forking out for costly alarms.
- Make your fitness equipment.
- Learn to DIY around the house.
- Stock up on dried and canned foods a little at a time.

# CHAPTER 2: PREPPER'S MINDSET

**Preparation Mentality**

Panic is a disease. It kills more people than any virus, fire, or flood. Panic convinces us that guns are more important than food. It forces us to trample on others to get what we need. Panic makes us dumb. Stupidity is lethal.

How do we stay calm? The only way to avoid panic is to plan ahead of time. Preparation is about being confident that you will have the necessities for survival and a reason to keep pushing, adapting, and thriving. Preparation ensures that your focus is always on how to make the best of a bad situation, rather than facing it with no plan at all.

Preparing for a natural or man-made disaster is not crazy, conspiracy theorist, or overly zealous. It is a fundamental aspect of human evolution. You prepare for a job interview or an exam the same way our forefathers had to prepare for a hunt or war. We play out scenarios in our heads, preparing our bodies for the task at hand. The greatest test of our lives is the need to survive, and if you're reading this, you're aware of your role in any extreme emergency.

# PREPPER'S LONG-TERM SURVIVAL GUIDE

It's not about frantically gathering everything you can in anticipation of the future. It's about focusing on what you can do right now to maintain your health and normalcy, regardless of what happens in the future. More than that, it's about better equipping yourself to serve your family, friends, and community.

The sense of community that comes with a disaster is something you won't find in any other survival guide. You'll only find fear-based advice telling you to keep to yourself and trust no one. You only hear about the terrible looting and hoarding and how being prepared may make you a target for being mugged or killed.

## Mental Health Survival Guide

After experiencing significant traumatic experiences, it is "natural" to struggle to maintain control over one emotion. However, if one chooses to ignore the stress and let it build up, it may have a negative impact on both one mental and physical health. The following is a list of suggestions for coping strategies in these trying times:

***Discuss the situation:*** By talking about it with other people, one can relieve tension and become aware that others share one's feelings.

***Spend time with family and close friends:*** They can help you get through this difficult time. If the oner family lives elsewhere, keep in touch with them by phone. If you have children, you must encourage them to talk to you about their concerns and how they are feeling about the disaster.

***Make a point of looking for yourself:*** Make sure to get enough sleep, stay active, and eat a healthy diet. If you smoke cigarettes or drink coffee, try to limit how much you do it because nicotine and caffeine both contribute to increased stress.

Reduce the number of times people are shown photographs of the disaster: Repeatedly seeing or reading news coverage of the traumatic event will only make one feel more stressed.

***Make time for the things that bring you joy:*** Spend some time relaxing by watching a movie, taking a walk, reading a book, or doing anything else that makes you happy. These physically active pursuits may assist in diverting one's attention away from the disaster and lowering one's stress level.

***First, let us concentrate on one issue at a time:*** When someone is already stressed, even a normal amount of work may seem insurmountable at times. Please select the most pressing issue and get to work on it. After completing that assignment, you should move on to the next one. When one "checks off" the chores on one list, it gives one a sense of accomplishment and makes things seem less daunting.

***Take some positive steps:*** Donate blood, assemble "care packages" for people who have lost loved ones, homes, or jobs, or volunteer your time to aid in the recovery and restoration efforts. When one is in a situation that appears "out of one's control," helping others may give one a sense of purpose.

***Avoid using drugs and binge drinking:*** In the short term, substances like alcohol or drugs may provide the illusion of stress relief, but in the long run, they almost always produce other issues that add to the stress that a person is already experiencing. When you find yourself in a jam, seek help.

You already know if you're a survivalist or prepper, but if you're new to the mindset, here are a few pointers on improving your life.

# PREPPING FUNDAMENTALS

### 1. Recognize the Triggers

These are the events that would prompt you to begin preparing for a disaster or emergency. Everyone is different in terms of what they can and cannot handle.

Some see it as an economic downturn that could result in mass unemployment. For others, it could be credit card debt, a family disease, or anything else.

It all depends on your situation and allows you to decide how to prepare.

### 2. When's and Where's

Choose the type of scenario that would prompt you to prepare.

There are various scenarios, each of which is more realistic than the others.

### 3. The How-To's

**Determine how much preparation you will do**

This is the most important part; it is entirely up to you. If you want to do more, that's fine, as long as you're capable of handling everything and have a solid support system in place.

**Each individual will determine this**

The most important thing is to make sure that everyone in your family understands how your preparation will affect them. If something happens to one of you while prepping and your needs are not met, he or she may become angry at the other family members and refuse to help them simply because they are prepping.

**Begin making preparations now so that nothing can end your life while you are preparing**

This is the most difficult part; it will take time and effort. You must be persistent in your preparation, even if you do not see immediate results. They will come to you if you always care for your needs.

There is no such thing as a perfect prepper, but there are things that can be done to make sure that everything can be accomplished with the least amount of preparation.

**Preppers' Equipment's Checklist**

If you are a prepper, then you know the importance of being prepared for any disaster. Be sure to always have the necessary tools and gear for survival in an emergency.

The following is the list of items that each preparer needs to survive:

A knife or multirole, like a Swiss army knife or Leatherman tool, is essential for making tasks easier when the worse comes to worst. A sharp tool that will allow you to quickly work tasks such as chopping wood, setting traps, or opening cans of food can make an enormous difference. A knife or multirole is also important for self-defense, so be sure to keep it within reach at all times.

Hand protection is important for comfort and safety in any situation. Gloves will protect your hands from cuts, scrapes, abrasions, and the cold. Be sure to have a good pair of waterproof gloves in case you need them for the weather conditions that you are preparing for or even just for dirty tasks like gathering firewood or cleaning fish and game.

A quality first-aid kit is essential for your health and your family's health in case of an emergency. It should include bandages, gauze, and antibiotic ointment. And other equipment that will keep you healthy and safe. Be sure to have enough medicine on hand for any injuries you or another family member might encounter.

# PREPPER'S LONG-TERM SURVIVAL GUIDE

Medicine is important no matter what kind of situation you are preparing for. Stock up on some aspirin, ibuprofen, and antacids to have on hand for any aches or pains that you might experience. Be sure to take any medication only when absolutely necessary so that it will last longer.

A radio that can pick up AM, FM, and shortwave bands is important for staying informed about any emergency situations or learning about local weather conditions. You could even pick up a shortwave radio to listen in on other countries in case of an emergency. Many shortwave radios can also act as a flashlight or power source.

Flashlights are essential for any situation, from finding your way around when it is dark to finding your things during an emergency evacuation. Make sure that you have flashlights for every room in your house and that they all work properly when you need them most.

Portable power is important for keeping electronics charged when the power goes out. Car chargers are important so you can keep your cell phone or other portable devices charged in an emergency. You can also use a solar-powered charger to keep your batteries and devices charged while on the go so that you will always have access to information from radio stations or electronic devices like your GPS.

A compass is important for navigation. The earth's magnetic field points north, so it can be used to tell which way you should head if you get lost or need to navigate around obstacles during an emergency situation.

Headlamps are useful in inclement weather conditions and can also be used to light up rooms, paths, etc. when it is dark outside.

Water is essential to keep you healthy and hydrated. Be sure to have plenty of clean drinking water that does not need purification at all times so that you will never run out of water during an emergency or while on the go. You may want to stock up on water bottles if you have the room because they are easy to store and carry around wherever you go.

Fire is required for survival in many situations. Having emergency matches or a lighter on hand will ensure that you will always be able to start a fire when needed. You should also have at least one fire extinguisher on hand in case a fire breaks out at home or on the go. Be sure to practice how to use it properly to save lives and property whenever possible.

Shelter is important for protection against the elements and keeping your family safe. A tent and/or sleeping bags will allow you to move from place to place easily or stay warm in inclement weather conditions if you have to evacuate your home.

Waterproof bags are important for keeping your belongings dry, especially if you have to evacuate your home. They can also be used to keep electronics dry if you are on the go and need to protect them from water.

A watch or wristwatch is important for helping you keep track of the time, especially during emergency situations when it may be difficult to know what time it is. It will also help you keep up with the past and understand how many days have passed since the disaster occurred or after the disaster was announced. In addition, wristwatches can also be used as tools for survival in case of an emergency.

**Important Documents**

Always keep a copy of important documents, such as prescriptions, birth certificates, and other necessary paperwork, in a waterproof container on hand. This will make replacing these documents easier if they are lost or destroyed during an emergency or major disaster. I also have a copy of my will, insurance policy, and passport in my bug-out bag.

Keep important family documents, such as passports, wills, and other legal papers, in waterproof containers as well. It's also a good idea to keep extra copies of these items at home in case they need to be replaced. Family photos are also useful in an emergency because they can aid in identification.

Make a copy of your life insurance policy, retirement plan, and other important documents and keep them in a waterproof container. Additionally, keep photocopies of these documents at home. Keep a copy of your birth certificate at home and photocopies in case of an emergency or if the ID is required for survival. Additionally, keep extra copies of this document at home so that they can be replaced or used if the original document is destroyed during an emergency.

Keep copies of your driver's license, passport, and other important documents in a waterproof container, along with copies of your medical records and prescription information. These are always with me, as are copies of my health insurance card and prescriptions.

Always keep a copy of your life insurance policy and other important paperwork on hand, especially if you use it to protect property by ensuring that it is properly insured. These papers are kept in an emergency kit or are easily accessible for reference if needed.

More than anything else, photocopies or digital images of important documents such as prescriptions, passports, and social security cards should be kept in an easily accessible location.

Document your important documents and keep copies in a waterproof container in a secure location. This way, even if you have a copy of the most important document, you can use it with confidence in case the original is damaged.

I hope this will help you in making sure that your papers are secure, easily available, and protected from damage during an emergency situation. These paper documents could matter more than any electronic documents you may have stored on a computer or electronic device like a tablet or smartphone because if they are lost or destroyed during an emergency, it will be impossible for anyone to access them from their location without your paperwork.

## How to Prepare Your Family for Strenuous Situations

Home is the safest place to build what you want. Things can be stored indefinitely. The home must be built accordingly for a short-term plan of less than three months. One can create a safe room in their home to help them, and their families hide during a disaster. Under Earth, one can build anything, such as a storeroom where one can keep necessary items to help one survive during long and short-term plans. The home structure is critical for creating such places. Even during the war, one can seek refuge in the secret basement to save their family's life. One can store as many items as one wants. Food storage is dependent on management and does not rely on empty spaces. Numerous ideas can help one store the most important things in the least amount of space, such as storing multiple kitchen utensils in a wooden box or a plastic bag. Similarly, one can keep as many clothes as they want. As a result, it is up to the individual to organize the space according to capacity.

One must understand the benefits of storing things before a disaster because one will be unable to manage things after a disaster. A person can survive without proper food and water, but a family cannot survive without proper water and food. Assume you have children and need milk for them. It will be extremely difficult to arrange milk and properly feed the children. If one has elderly parents in the family, they may require soft food, which will be difficult to arrange during a disaster or emergency. To keep children and elderly parents healthy, proper food is always required.

A medical first aid kit, important kitchen utensils, important electric gadgets, an electricity backup plan, water storage, food storage, clothes, space for fresh air, a bathroom, and space for laundry are all required. These are important things to build and store for both short and long periods.

- When does your family face a difficult situation?
- What kinds of things might be difficult for kids to deal with in a stressful situation?
- What can you do to prepare your family for situations like this?

Making this process more enjoyable for your child will increase their likelihood of preparing for these situations. Tell them they will be rewarded if they keep everything organized and ready to go before leaving.

We understand. It's difficult to imagine what might happen in the event of a disaster. But who knows how your family will react if you don't prepare them for these events now?

This will cover everything you'll need to know when preparing your family for a disaster: what disasters are most likely in your area; how to assess and organize your home and property; what gear is necessary for survival; and more. Furthermore, we will provide you with some helpful guidelines for preparing children so that they are not scared during an emergency.

The first step is to assess the risk that your home faces from natural disasters and man-made hazards by completing the following steps: View an interactive map that shows the likelihood of each type of hazard in your area.

- Examine the physical aspects of your home.
- Inspect the structure of your home to see if it can withstand the force of a hurricane or other severe storms.
- Examine your structure for any flaws that could expose it to fire, floods, or earthquakes.
- Examine your property that is related to the house.
- Examine the pipes and power lines that lead to your house.
- Examine your insurance and other plans.

Get a home insurance policy before you make any purchases. Consider purchasing extra supplies from Home Depot or Amazon based on how likely you believe you will encounter those hazards. Before having them delivered and ready to use, compare your purchase to what you require.

Make sure your area has emergency plans in place. Then, recall the list of potential hazards in your area to get an idea of what disasters are most likely to occur there. People in California, for example, should be more concerned about wildfires or earthquakes than flooding, whereas Floridians should be concerned about hurricanes.

**Survival Skills for Children and the Elderly**

If you live in a city or ever have to leave your home with nothing but what you're wearing on your back, these survival skills could save your life. Whether it's an earthquake, a 9/11-like terrorist attack, or just the next big blizzard that's touched down in the Northeast and is headed for the rest of us soon (and we all know that will happen eventually), you'll need some skills to get through it. People frequently do not take the time to learn about survival skills because it may not appear necessary—but look at Hurricane Katrina in 2005 and tell me how wrong they are. There are some things you should know ahead of time in order to survive an emergency like this.

# PREPPING FUNDAMENTALS

The most important message you can give a child is, "Don't be afraid of being afraid." They should not run away from the fear but rather recognize that it is normal to be afraid and then take action. When you're in an uncomfortable or unfamiliar situation, it's natural to be afraid. Fear is what keeps people alive in the first place. Their fear causes them to avoid dangerous situations and, as a result, stay alive.

All of these abilities are intended to save lives, particularly those of children. If you don't know what to teach them, choose one and get started. If you are pressed for time, make it a family project and teach your child how to do it with your assistance.

With the rise in senior care, those caring for aging relatives must be prepared to provide the necessities to ensure their survival.

## Developing Children's Emergency Preparedness

As a parent, there is perhaps nothing more stressful than discovering that a calamity has struck and that you have not been adequately prepared.

Our children are considerably more vulnerable to disasters than we are, both physically and emotionally, and it is our responsibility to ensure that they are able to survive them successfully.

All areas of disaster preparedness with children, from infancy through adolescence, are covered in detail in this guide.

## Infants Disaster Preparedness

The first year of a child's life is brief, and there is already so much stress around the new arrival that you may be tempted to overlook disaster preparation for your small child.

Infants, on the other hand, are far more vulnerable to disasters than adults or even little children. Because of their weakened immune systems, even minor incidences of water pollution or an infected wound might result in the death of these people.

Even when the newborn is not in immediate danger, I've witnessed parents panic out because they are worried about their child during emergencies. If you have supplies and a strategy in place, you will be more prepared to deal with a crisis.

# BOOK 2:
# BUG-IN: YOUR HOME IS YOUR GREATEST SURVIVAL SHELTER

## BUG IN
# YOUR HOME IS YOUR GREATEST SURVIVAL SHELTER

Staying put may be the best course of action if traveling is too risky or if you are adequately prepared for whatever disaster, you are now confronted with within your present area. In order to bug in, you must be prepared to bunker down and "ride out" the ordeal.

It may be best to remain there if traveling is too hazardous or you are adequately prepared for whatever disaster you are experiencing in your present area. You're ready to bunker down and "ride it out" if you're bugging in.

When it comes to major supplies like food and water, this is where bugging in beats bugging out: you can stock up on essential supplies like food, water, medicines, and others like weapons, ammunition, and other important equipment. While your BOB should be as light as possible, ruling out stuffing it with canned goods for food, you can fill up your pantry and attic with enough food to tide you over for long periods until the government can bring peace and order back to your city. You also have the benefit of sleeping in your own bed and being protected from the elements.

Stock up on foods with long shelf lives, like canned goods, uncooked rice, and clean drinking water. In particular, aim for at least a month's worth. You'll never know how long it will take before the government can put things under control and normalize the situation after a disaster has plummeted your city into anarchy and chaos.

Stock up on fire extinguishers as well to help keep your home safe from fires in case one breaks out accidentally.

**Checklist for Bugging-in Essentials**

The primary distinction between bugging out and bugging in preparation is the number of supplies available. You won't have to worry about where you'll get your supplies if you stay prepared. When it comes to breaking in, your only limitation is the amount of available space.

Food for the unanticipated. You should make healthier dietary choices while bugging in. Make sure you have a large supply of the best types of emergency food for your situation.

In an emergency, water is required. Check to see if you have a reliable emergency water supply. Preparing an emergency water plan ensures that you always have access to water, no matter what happens.

**First-aid supplies**

Make sure you have a good first aid kit and a basic understanding of basic medical abilities with you.

Light and heat are available as backups. Keep a supply of batteries, flashlights, and lanterns on hand. A generator is a wise investment if you have the space.

**Likely Bug-in Scenarios**

Depending on the circumstances, any of the situations mentioned in the bug-out part may also be grounds for a bug-in. You'll have to weigh the pros and cons of remaining or leaving based on the specifics of the scenario. Some of these situations will be included in the bug-out part, although some significant variations in the situation's details.

The economy is in free fall. While serious economic hardship may lead to rioting and other human issues, bugging in is preferable if you're self-sufficient and can properly protect your house and stockpile. This is particularly true for rural preppers, but many city preppers can handle it as well. Bugging in makes the greatest sense if you can go off the grid, grow your food, and defend your location against looters for the long haul.

A viral epidemic has occurred. Depending on the severity of the virus epidemic, leaving your house may be too hazardous owing to the risk of infection. This is particularly true if the disease is spread via the air. If the virus is airborne, duct tape & plastic sheeting may be necessary to keep you safe inside your house.

A chemical or biological assault is possible. If a chemical or biological terrorist attack occurs, staying inside may be preferable and waiting it out. Another scenario in which exposing oneself to the outdoor air may be fatal. Take anthrax, for example; this lethal weapon may be disseminated over a wide population and kill anybody who goes outdoors and breathes it in.

Nuclear calamity. In general, it's preferable to avoid fallout as soon as feasible. However, if things move too quickly and the afflicted region is so large that you might not be able to evade the radiation without suffering fatal effects, you'll have to stay put. If you don't make it out of the catastrophe in time, you might have no option but to bunker down and wait it out.

Unrest in the streets. Rioting and looting events may happen out of nowhere. Being caught outdoors as the crowds' swell may result in severe injury or death. A sharp eye can notice the warning signals before they become dangerous, but you can't constantly be on the lookout. It's better to remain put if there's a lot of aggressive action going on outside your door. Reconsider if leaving out is a smart option after the movement has subsided before another wave arrives.

Natural calamity. While many natural catastrophes may be anticipated, you might well find yourself in a position where you are unable to escape before things get dangerous. If a natural catastrophe is already happening and obstructing your escape path, bugging in may be the best choice. Humans are soft and breakable, to put it simply. Stay inside and bunker down unless your area is at immediate risk of destruction.

This should be self-evident, but I'll point it out nonetheless. Stay put if you don't have a safe location to bug out or if your safe place has been compromised. You're better off staying in than roaming around unless your present position is at risk or your resources are depleted.

**Self Defense**

If you and your family decide to stay and hold the fort, this will be your top priority. Disasters have the ability to neutralize government law enforcement, even if only for a short time, resulting in anarchy and chaos - everyone for himself or herself. Expect criminality to be the order of the day in such situations in the name of survival. Those who are unprepared become the targets of the prepared.

There are some things you can do to reduce your chances of encountering nasty things from desperate people during disasters that can paralyze government operations. Keep in mind that these are only guidelines and suggestions and should not be regarded as absolute truths. Finally, in the event of an urban disaster, you should use your discretion as to how to apply this in your specific situation and environment.

**Darkness Rules**

By boarding your windows and, to the greatest extent possible, turning off your lights at night, you can avoid attracting the special attention and interest of looters or other criminal elements. When the entire metropolis is in darkness due to a lack of power, even the smallest of lights can easily attract the attention of undesirable elements.

## Strengthen the Fortress
Secure your home as much as you can from the inside so that you don't draw too much attention from the outside. To secure your home's entry and exit points, reinforce the doors with extra bolts, door jammers, chain locks, and barricades. If they aren't enough to deter intruders, they can at least slow them down long enough for you to escape through the backdoor or prepare to take them down.

## The more people who band together, the more secure you will be
As much as possible, collaborate with your neighbors and community to build a strong bond while there is no disaster. Close relationships with your neighbors provide access to assistance when needed, better protection for everyone from unwanted people, and a lower risk of them targeting you for personal survival. It's also your best long-term disaster survival option.

## Make your home unattractive
This may seem blasphemous to many supporters of the beautiful home tenet but bear with me. By making your home appear unattractive or unassuming from the outside, i.e., not built like a palace or a fortress, you make it less noticeable and an unattractive target for looters, gangs, or desperate people looking for food or other supplies.

Suppose you don't want to bug out and prefer to stay home and batten down the hatches. In that case, you'll need to learn how to do it well to enhance your chances of survival, especially if disaster brings anarchy and mayhem until government troops can restore order. This is especially essential considering that most of the country's population lives in cities and other densely populated places. That means there will be more urgent competition for life supplies, posing a greater risk.

# BOOK 3: FOOD

## FOOD

# CHAPTER 1: HOW TO ORGANIZE YOUR PANTRY AND SUPPLIES - THE PREPPER'S PANTRY

Figuring out how to store food for a long has helped individuals for quite a long time, starting with families who had storage spaces or larders. In those days, long-term food storage was a need, as it was the best way to keep dinners new without refrigeration like we have today.

In present-day culture, planning food for long-term storage can be an excellent method for endurance during crises. It is energetically suggested that each family consider having a sufficient stockpile set to the side to keep going for a couple of months.

Begin with the objective of having a multi-month supply of foods you routinely appreciate.

If you have forever been interested in having your own food storeroom with enough holds for your family and an adequate measure of additional items, this guide will be vital to you.

**Necessary Equipment and Tools for Food Storage**

Several kinds of tools and equipment are used in the packaging and preservation of food items for storage. Basic kitchen equipment like knives, trays, cutting boards, colanders, measuring cups and spoons of different sizes, funnels, and weighing scales will be needed to make the different commodities into appropriate storage forms.

The major tools are those directly involved in storage and preservation and can be used for both short-term and long-term purposes. Most of these are simple tools such as metal cans, plastic buckets, etc. General precautions to take with these containers include washing them with warm water and soap and drying them thoroughly. We don't want to risk contamination of the stored foods or contact with water because microorganisms can grow in the smallest amount of moisture.

If you intend to stock dry food supplies, you will require special containers to keep all ingredients fresh and the storage counters organized. They are your emergency supplies and require proper storage that includes maximum durability, tight sealing, and easy identification. Without such containers, your prepper pantry will become out of control, and the quality of your food may suffer as a result. You can select from the following container types:

Plastic containers are made of polyester, polycarbonate, polyethylene, and other materials. They are the most commonly used containers for storing dry goods. Plastic containers are an option if you are preparing your food pantry and want to stock up on dry goods for long-term storage.

***Metal Cans***—Metal cans can be used to store dry foods. However, they are significantly more expensive than plastic ones. This is because metal cans require specialized equipment to store food in them. Metal cans are not as accountable as other popular solutions, but they can rust if not properly maintained.

***Vacuum Pouch***—While vacuum pouches are less durable, they have the potential to keep food fresh for a longer period. You can store dry foods in it and seal the pouch to keep the contents fresh. You can get a variety of sizes to accommodate your dry foods.

***Jars made of glass***—Glass jars are thought to be more stable than metal cans. However, glass jars are fragile and cannot withstand accidental falls or bumps. The advantage of using glass jars is that they can be reused numerous times.

# PREPPER'S LONG-TERM SURVIVAL GUIDE

The ability of a container to prevent the entry of bacteria and mold formation in food determines its effectiveness. The container's construction should be strong, light, and leakproof. When storing dry foods in them, you should invest in an airtight container. You can choose the sizes and shapes based on how much dry food you want to store. Finally, make sure the materials are food-grade! It will keep your food from becoming contaminated while it is stored in it.

Dishwashing liquid soap solutions and a cleaning brush are required for treating or cleaning containers of all types. Simply pour your dishwashing liquid into the container, pour some water over it, and turn off the water. Scrub the container from all sides with the brush, then rinse it clean with water. Your dry food storage containers have been treated and cleaned.

## Prepping the Pantry

Indeed, you should not count on taste as a priority when gathering survival food for the pantry. But still, you need to note what your family would prefer to eat in the worst survival state. The smarter idea is to decide upon cheap food products that keep you full for a longer time. Talk to your family members and prepare the list before making your purchase. You would not want to waste your money and pantry space on foods that no one would even like to eat for survival!

The top five items that are a must for your prepper pantry are:

- Grains
- Beans
- Oil
- Water
- Canned/Dried Produce

## Keep the Food Fresh

All the food you keep on hand will not last forever and will have an expiry date. As a result, you should adhere to the FIFO (First In, First Out) strategy used by restaurants and cafes to keep their stocks fresh. To keep the cycle going, you must use the pantry items and replace them with new ones.

Assume you're using a rice pack from your pantry that you've had for a long time. In that case, you must bring in a new pack to replace the one you previously used.

You should begin with food and water storage by following these steps. The best thing you can do right away is to make a list of items you might need in an emergency. As a newcomer to the concept of prepping, keep in mind that you do not need to panic and rush into stockpiling edible goods. Cover all of the essential chapters in this book, and you'll have a good idea of how to start, proceed, and set up the prepper pantry.

## Tracking the Pantry

The key to maintaining and rotating your pantry is staying organized. Keep a list of all your items and write down their package dates. Some preppers write the package date in large letters directly on the item as well, so they don't need to refer to their master list every time. You can also set reminders in a digital calendar, so you'll be notified when a date is coming up.

As soon as you use an item, write it on a list, so you know you need to replace it. Do you need to replace it right away? You don't need to make a special trip to the store to get a single can of toma-

# FOOD

toes, but don't wait too long. You want your stockpile as complete as possible at all times because you don't know when an emergency might arise.

## Essential Foods to Have Inside the Pantry

Foods may be perishable or non-perishable. As these terms suggest, perishable foods do not last so long as non-perishable foods, which may stay unspoiled for years. This variation in lifespans is because food items have different nutrient content. The amount of water and oil in a portion of food appears to be the most important factor in determining longevity. The less of these two presents in a commodity, the greater the chances of them staying long on the shelf.

## Grains

### Soft and Hard Grains

When it comes to essential foods that last a long time, grains like rice are the first to come to mind, owing to their low water content. Soft grains like quinoa, barley, and rye, as well as hard grains like wheat and millet, can be stored for up to 8-10 years. They may even last longer if properly protected in airtight storage containers, particularly those obtained from stores and supermarkets that sell food in long-term storage.

White rice, in particular, can be stored properly for up to twenty years.

## Pasta

The key concept behind long-lasting foods is that they contain little to no moisture. The various types of pasta fit the bill. Those obtained from retail stores should not be used after their two-year shelf life. However, some, particularly dry ones, can survive for up to ten years. They really do last that long.

## Hardtack

Hardtacks, also known as pilot bread and ship bread, may not be as appealing as brown cakes, but they must be included in this venerable group of long-lasting foods. They are nearly indestructible and have been a staple food on ships for decades. During the American Civil War, they were even given to soldiers as food. Furthermore, depending on your imagination, they can be easily made from readily available ingredients such as flour and flour, and possibly salt or sugar.

## Flours

Flours, particularly those made from wheat, can be extremely durable, lasting for decades. However, they are better stored unground because grinding drastically reduces their longevity. You should keep them as grains and only powder them when necessary.

## Oatmeal, Rolled

Oatmeal is the most common form of oat and is usually sold in cans. As long as storage guidelines are followed, canned oatmeal can last for about 1-2 years, depending on the manufacturer. The most important rules are to keep them at room temperature and away from moisture or oxygen in a cool, dry place. It is always a good idea to store water-sensitive foods with oxygen absorbers.

## Proteins

### Beans

Beans are one of the most valuable food items in many countries because they are the cheapest source of protein. Several cultures combine beans and rice in novel and interesting ways to provide protein and fiber. They can last for up to 5 years if dried or canned. They will be fine if kept sealed away with oxygen absorbers. Dried beans, on the other hand, become extremely difficult after 5 years because they typically require longer periods of cooking. Because of the risk of botulism, canned beans, like other canned foods, should not be used after their expiration dates.

### Meats

Meats come in a variety of varieties and can be preserved in a variety of ways. The majority of meats are either fresh, lightly dried, freeze-dried, or canned. While fresh meat appears to be the best delicacy, it cannot be relied on in the long run. This is why, when it comes to storing meat, the best option is to dry it yourself. You can then vouch for the preserve's integrity. In any case, dried meats are widely available in stores and supermarkets, and they typically have a shelf life of about two years under normal storage conditions. On the other hand, freeze-dried meats can last up to 15 years.

Depending on the manufacturer, canned meats such as corn beef, spam, and chicken can be indestructible for 1-5 years. To avoid unpleasant surprises, always check that the cans are intact.

### Lentils

Lentils, which belong to the legume family, are high in protein and fiber. They, like beans, usually do not last more than five years in their dried form.

### Eggs

Oh, the eggs! They elevate the food and stimulate the taste buds in their natural state. You'll have to settle for powdered form if you want them for a long time. Powdered eggs must be purchased from a reputable long-term storage manufacturer. If stored properly, they can last up to ten years.

### Pemmican

Pemmican is a powdered mixture of lean, dried meat and melted fat. They aren't particularly tasty, but they can come in handy in a pinch. They can last for 4-5 decades if properly stored. Surprised? That is not a myth.

### Butters made from nuts

Groundnuts and butter combined. They, too, stay for a while because they are always good and ready to eat.

We can talk about 15 years in powdered form. However, don't get your hopes up when they're in glass jars. After about 24 months, they usually give up.

## Vegetables and fruits

Fruits and vegetables like cabbage and broccoli, as well as roots like onion and potato, are rich in vitamins, fiber, and other essential nutrients.

### Fruits, Dried

Fruits taste best when they are raw and unprocessed. Nothing beats that flavor, especially when you're munching on your favorite. However, just like other foods, they must lose moisture if they are to last for an extended time. Dehydrated apples, strawberries, and other fruits can last for about

20 years if properly dehydrated. Like other food items, reliably dehydrated fruits can only be obtained from companies that manufacture long-term foods.

### Fruits Freeze-Dried

Lyophilization and cryodesiccation are other terms for freeze-drying. When stored properly, freeze-dried fruits can last nearly as long as dried fruits.

### Fruits in Cans

Canned fruits keep their delicious taste for a long time, and manufacturers state that they can last for about 2-3 years. It is best to strictly adhere to storage instructions for maximum preservation.

### Vegetables, Dried

Salad, fruiting, shooting, and squash vegetables are all types of vegetables.

Others include roots like potatoes and bulbs like onions. They are delicious and safe sources of nutrition. Because of the differences in water content of individual vegetables, shelf lives in the fresh, unprocessed form are not the same. Dehydrated vegetables, on the other hand, can last for decades when dried.

Dried onions, for example, can be stored properly for up to ten years.

### Vegetables, Freeze-Dried

The average lifespan of freeze-dried vegetables is 5-10 years.

### Vegetables in Cans

If the manufacturer's storage instructions are strictly followed, canned foods can last for up to two years.

### Potato Flakes, Dried

Potatoes are most commonly stored in the form of flakes. These could last for up to 15 years. Simply keep it in a cool, dry place away from light.

### Corn Dried

Dried corn can last indefinitely. This is especially true when not exposed to water or moisture.

### Leather Fruit

Fruit rolls, also known as fruit rolls, are an ingenious way humans have devised to preserve fruits. These fruit snacks will keep in the freezer for about a year.

## Oils

### Cocoa Butter

Coconut oil can be stored in airtight containers for up to 1-5 years. When they are exposed, they will not be able to hold out for that long. Oils turn rancid when they are spoiled, making it difficult to detect when they are no longer usable.

### Extra Virgin Olive Oil

Olive oil, like coconut oil, has a shelf life of about 2-5 years. They must be kept cool and dry, and at room temperature. If you notice that they have gone rancid, do not use them.

### Butter Clarified

This is also known as ghee and is commonly used in cooking. You can keep them unopened for about 2 years. They can be kept at room temperature or refrigerated.

## Other Necessities

Tea This one item appears to be eternal. It has been stealing its way into the menus of many families since time immemorial, thanks to its numerous health benefits. Manufacturers commonly sell them in bags; your beverage is safe for about 2 years.

### Coffee

It appears that beverages do not want to be spoiled. Coffee, both instant and freeze-dried, can be stored for more than 20 years. If kept in a freezer, they can last for years.

Powdered cocoa can be stored in airtight containers for up to two years, possibly longer.

### Milk

Milk should be stored in dry, airtight containers as a powder. They could last for 15 years or more in this condition. When improperly preserved, they, like oils, begin to smell rancid, indicating that they are no longer fit for consumption.

### Honey

Raw honey has nutritional benefits in addition to making food sweet. They can, thankfully, be left intact for years as long as they do not come into contact with water. However, they may crystallize after a while. This isn't a problem because all you have to do is soak them in warm water to get your honey back.

### Sugar

As a sweetener, sugar, like honey, is used. To last as long as possible, they must be kept dry and cool, away from light. Sugar attracts all kinds of ants, so make every effort to keep it out of reach of these hardworking crustaceans.

### Syrups

Maple syrup and corn syrup can be stored for as long as possible in the store. Store in airtight containers in a cool, dry place. They should be kept refrigerated or frozen to extend their shelf life.

### Salt

The greatest seasoning agent of all time is salt. Because it is a well-known preservative, it does not require any special preservation techniques. It is safe to keep at home indefinitely. However, it must be ensured that it is not contaminated with poisonous agents. Because it may attract moisture from the surrounding environment, it should be stored in airtight containers. Unprocessed salts, such as Himalayan salt, are ideal. Alcohol, vinegar, herbs, spices, bouillon, soy sauce, and baking soda are among the other foods.

## How Long Can You Store Food?

It's vital to know how long you can store food appropriately. Food can be stored for different time spans, contingent upon what you have decided to add to your reserve.

Some food things, like dry beans and white rice, will endure significantly longer than new greens. This is particularly obvious if you expect that you will not approach refrigeration in an emergency. The essential target of getting all of the ideal foods for long-term storage is to think about their best-by dates. What's more, you need to consider the different ways of helping them keep going significantly longer than on a supermarket rack.

## FOOD

You will track down foods that last as long as 90 days, though others can stay palatable for a really long time. This is fundamental for mortgage holders who need to accumulate sufficient long-term food storage.

If you're picking more medium-term storage, ordinarily as long as 90 days, you can zero in additional on fulfilling and ameliorating dinners as opposed to foods loaded with fundamental nutrients and minerals.

Long-term food storage is intended to keep going for a really long time. These incorporate fixings with a period of usability of 25 years for however long they are appropriately bundled.

The comfort of approaching a cooler during an emergency would be incomprehensibly helpful, particularly as there's no assurance when your power will go out. Nonetheless, only one out of every odd family is keen on planning for endurance. They might be just interested with regards to how long their #1 foods can last when refrigerated.

To guarantee you don't make yourself sick with destructive microorganisms, we utilized graphs to look into the refrigerated lifespan of most foods.

Refrigerated at 40°F or underneath Food Type Refrigeration Period Crude Pork 3 to 5 days Crude Poultry 1 to 2 days Crude Beef 1 to 2 days Soups and Stews 3 to 4 days Eggs 3 to 5 weeks Leftovers 3 to 4 days Lunch Meats 2 weeks (unopened)

Frozen at 0°F or beneath Food Type Frozen Period Crude Pork 4 to a year Crude Poultry 1 year Crude Beef 3 to 4 months (ground), 4 to a year (steaks) Soup and Stews 2 to 90 days Eggs Do not freeze Leftovers 2 to a half-year Lunch Meats 1 to 2 months

**How to Organize Your Pantry?**

When stockpiling food and water supplies in your prepper pantry, you should organize them so that you can easily find them during an emergency. For example, if you need some ready-to-eat snacks, you should have direct access to the container where you originally stored them. You should not have to rummage through different food boxes to find the one you require. As a result, this is something that occurs when you are disorganized.

When a disaster is approaching, and you only have a few days to respond, you may not be able to access any of the resources or stocks in supermarkets and local stores because last-minute preppers will rush to the markets and get their goods on a first-come, first-served basis. And it is at this point that latecomer will run out of supplies to last the duration of the disaster and its aftermath. As a result, you must act quickly and with a sense of responsibility when organizing the supplies.

Whether you have a small or large supply set, you must organize them all effectively so that you can access necessary items when needed. For example, if someone has a severe allergic reaction, you must have immediate access to anti-allergic medications to save that person's life. Imagine not being able to locate the medicine box in your storage area! Things could get out of hand! Similarly, if you have a baby during a disaster, they will require a variety of foods. And you must be available to all of them throughout the survival period to ensure your baby's healthy survival.

Only keep the foods you eat. One of the avoidable mistakes that preppers make is stockpiling on everything that catches their eye. Amateur preppers are concerned with simply gathering food, regardless of whether they intend to eat it. They buy everything else they see in the supermarket! They prefer to buy and stock items that appear edible and shelf-stable over time. But this is a completely incorrect approach! You should only stockpile food and beverages that you intend to consume even during the worst of times.

Spending money on unwanted foods will cause a new financial crisis in your family. You may desire to stock your refrigerator and storage pantry with food supplies throughout the year to be prepared for various unexpected threats. However, you should be cautious about what you intend to purchase!

Utilize Heavy-Duty Shelving Aside from stocking up on food, you should also make the necessary arrangements for adequate shelving. If you want to keep your food in a higher space and away from water leakage and pests, invest in heavy-duty shelves that will help you maximize storage space. You can choose between metal shelves and durable plastic shelves, both of which provide the necessary strength and ease of cleaning over time.

Furthermore, these shelves should be able to withstand the weight that is placed on them. When purchasing canned goods and food buckets for a survival stockpile, they are quite heavy. The most common organizing blunder is piling all of the supplies on the floor without properly arranging them. As a result, it creates a huge mess in the storage room, rendering the goods inaccessible during an emergency.

Aside from that, if you use low-quality or weaker shelves to store your food at a height, they will eventually fall apart, resulting in a lot of waste. Before deciding on a shelving material, double-check the manufacturer's specifications or the material's ability to withstand the weight of supplies.

Keep a Spreadsheet If your emergency food system is on a rotation system, you must remain at the top of the sheet. It means you should make a list or spreadsheet of the emergency supplies you have, what you have used from them, and what you need to replenish. This is the on-system organization of the prepper's pantry's survival food supplies. You do not need to prepare your spreadsheet with a pen and paper. Instead, you can keep track of it using your Excel Spreadsheet on your laptop. If you want a hard copy of the document, get a printout if you don't think you'll have access to your laptop during a crisis.

This organizational approach may not be the most brilliant, but it is unquestionably one of the most effective ways of ensuring that an adequate supply of emergency food is available at all times. Most inexperienced preppers prefer to consume supplies from their pantry's survival stocks that are about to expire. They then forget to replenish those supplies! As a result, when disaster strikes, they run out of food, putting your life and the lives of your family members at risk. The foods you use to rotate your supplies should be noted on the list and highlighted for restocking or refilling.

**Additional Food Pantry Organization Tips**

Aside from these obvious considerations, there are a few other important tips for seamless and organized food storage in your pantry:

*Group the Similar Items*—If you want to adapt the ease of finding the items even more conveniently during a crisis, keep the similar items nearby or together. For example, keep canned vegetables and beans together, dried mixes on the second shelf, and so on.

*Everything Will Be Labeled*—Without labels, it may be difficult to identify the boxes containing various items. It may irritate you in a time of need. When you are unable to recognize the boxes in an emergency, you will eventually panic. As a result, label everything, whether it's a small or large box, and don't be afraid to add a tag over it for its contents.

*Add More Shelves*—If there are any corners around the storage room or pantry that are rarely used, you can prefer to add more shelves to those corners. This will provide you with additional storage space around the room, allowing you to stock up on even more supplies.

*Have Some Tote Bags*—Tote bags are easy to handle, carry, or grab if you need to bug out quickly. Assume your vehicle isn't large enough to transport several tote bags. In that case, you can install a rooftop carrier over your vehicle to be prepared for emergency goods transportation. Pack heavy food items over the carriers to avoid overloading the vehicle. You can use the carrier to transport sleeping bags, clothing, and other small items. As a result, the space in your vehicle will be freed up for more food and drink supplies in the tote bags.

As a result, this is the best way to ensure proper food pantry organization. If you take all of these steps, you will be able to free up a lot of existing space within your storage sections. Use the remaining space to stockpile other survival necessities within the same room but a little further away from the food supplies. If there is any spillage, it might just cause damage and wastage of survival essentials. So, keep this factor in mind if you share the food storage room for other essentials.

# CHAPTER 2: LONG-TERM FOOD STORAGE METHODS

Short-term food storage is defined as preserving the food you tend to eat daily. These foods have a shorter shelf-life of around 3 to 5 years and are often purchased from the local grocery supermarkets or stores. On the other hand, the long-term storage is for the basic dry staples packaged for several years. The long-term storage foods are accountable for being preserved as survival pantry items, which can be edible and preserve nutrition for around 20 to 30 years.

# PREPPER'S LONG-TERM SURVIVAL GUIDE

The people new to this concept need a perfect differential understanding of how short-term and long-term storage varies. As you will be stocking up your emergency pantry with survival food items, you must know what you can store for a long- or short-time span.

**Short-Term Storage of Food**

Everything in your general kitchen pantry is for short-term food storage. These foods are rotated on a regular basis, and stocking up on them will help you deal with any short-term crisis. A well-stocked prepper pantry with food to last three months can assist your family in overcoming job loss, financial difficulties, food shortages, short-term illnesses, power outages, and natural disasters. Foods on the short-term food storage list have a shelf life of up to 5 years.

Canned foods can also be kept for 3 to 5 years. However, if they are stored in proper environmental conditions, you can eat them for an even longer time. However, there is an exception to this rule, as canned tomatoes are an example of highly acidic food that will not store for an extended period. Some canned food items to consider stocking up on in your prepper pantry include:

- Vegetables and fruits
- Chili, soups, and beans
- Meats
- Salsa, condiments, and pasta sauce
- Cooking with Peanut Butter Oil
- Jellies and jams

Aside from that, some packaged foods that you may want to include in your short-term food storage are:

- Ready-to-eat Cereal versus instant hot cereals
- Crackers, cookies, trail mix, fruit snacks, and chips are all available.
- Dried Fruits and Nuts
- Meats that have been smoked or dried, such as beef Jerky
- Cake mixes, brownie mixes, bread mixes, pancake mixes, and other baking mixes are examples of baking mixes.
- Pasta, rice, salt, spices, flour, and other staples
- Boxed Dinners like Macaroni and Cheese, Cooker Mixes, Pasta Mixes, Noodles, Dry Soup Mixes, and so on.
- Dressing, pasta, and gravy mixes are examples of packaged cooking mixes.
- Candy bars and chocolate chips
- Baby Cereal, Baby Formula, or Baby Food
- Sugar-free Desserts
- Pet food in cans
- Pet dry food
- Animal treats

You will require not only food but also beverages to survive. Aside from water, you should have some drinks on hand to deal with most crises or catastrophic events in the short term. Among the beverages are:

- Hot beverages
- Chocolate milk

# FOOD

- Teas made from herbs
- Substitutes for Tea Milk and Milk
- Sports beverages
- Mix of Soda, Fruit Juice, and Protein Drink
- Drink Mixes in Powder
- Nutrition Drinks or Meal Replacement Drinks

**Long-Term Storage of Food**

Long-term storage of food can be accountable as a rainy-day supply of food. These are considered the basic dry goods that are carefully stored to protect you from unforeseen challenges of the future. These long-term storage foods can offer you all the basic nutrition and calories for a survival scenario. Long-term food storage should act as a supplement to short-term food storage during tough times.

It is a strong investment that will help you safely pass any extended crisis. These food items are made up of dry goods with low oil and moisture. Therefore, these items can be stored for around 20 to 30 years. It is more like an insurance policy for your hunger needs amidst any crisis or long-term survival needs. If you run out of short-term supplies and the crisis doesn't end sooner than it should, you can rely upon these supplementary foods, which will give you the calories and nutrition you need.

The only important factor is that you need to give them sufficient time to make them edible. Most of the foods within the long-term storage are considered basic staples. Some specific long-term storage food items have just 10 years of shelf life, such as powdered dry milk (non-fat) or powdered eggs. With proper storage and preservation, the dry beans or grains that you store can last for over 25 to 30 years. The moisture content is accountable to be less than 10% in dry food to maximize shelf life.

Some of the dry goods that are ideal for long-term storage include:

- Wheat, Kamut, rolled oats, steel-cut oats, white rice, and other grains.
- Pasta varieties include elbow macaroni and spaghetti.
- Lentils, peas, and dry beans are examples of legumes.
- Sweet yellow corn, dent corn, flint corn, and other types of dried corn.
- Dried potatoes in the form of dice, slices, and flakes.
- Vegetables, both dried and freeze-dried.
- Baking with Salt Soda.
- Sugar, white.

Some of the dry goods that are preferable for long-term storage but have a shelf life of just 10 years are powdered dairy and powdered eggs.

**The Rotation of Long-Term Storage Food alongside the Short-Term Storage Food**

The basic survival strategy for storing food demands long-term and short-term storage food rotation with your regular diet. It is an ideal way of minimizing potential waste and ensuring the freshness of the food supply in your emergency pantry.

As a result, this is the most likely distinction between these two storage types. You must gain knowledge about stocking food supplies in their pantry. Whether you are storing food for the long or short term, your primary concern should be providing food security for your family in an emergency. The recent COVID pandemic has demonstrated the importance of a well-organized food system.

Rotating your stockpile is simple, but it does necessitate good organizational skills. You want to eat the food that is close to or has passed its expiration date and replace it. Why? In terms of nutrition, your stockpile will always be at its peak. While most foods can technically be consumed well after their "best by" date, they lose nutrients over time. You don't want to end up with a stockpile that is nutritionally deficient. You also don't want a stockpile that's so old that you're not sure what's safe to eat. Getting sick during a crisis is the last thing you want.

Digging into your stockpile on a regular basis also allows you to catch any storage issues before they destroy all of your supplies. In the long run, this saves you money. You'll also get to try some foods you don't normally eat to make sure you like them.

What about the element water? As we all know, water does not expire, but you always want your water to be as fresh as possible. Some preparedness experts advise rotating your water supply every year or so. You can use it for drinking, washing, or cooking before discarding it. This also allows you to check on your water to ensure that it has been properly stored. You don't have to worry too much if you forget to rotate a supply but know it's sealed and safe. Its freshness is more important than anything else.

**Fermentation**

In simple terms, fermentation is a metabolic process where the activity of microorganisms results in a change in food and drinks. This change is usually desirable as it adds flavor, increases health benefits, preserves food, and more. Although the word "ferment" is derived from the Latin word "fervere," which means "to boil," the fermentation process can occur without the presence of any heat.

Fermentation is an anaerobic process in which good microorganisms such as bacteria, yeast, and mold are present to obtain energy from fermentation.

In fact, when there is enough sugar, some yeast cells, such as Saccharomyces cerevisiae, prefer fermentation over aerobic respiration, even when there is plenty of oxygen. Good microbes break down starches and sugars into acids and alcohol during the fermentation process. This preserves food, allowing us to keep it for extended periods without it spoiling.

The enzymes produced by fermentation are also essential for digestion. Humans are born with a certain number of enzymes, which decreases as we age. Fermented foods provide us with the enzymes we need to break down foods. Fermentation also aids in pre-digestion. Microbes break down food before we consume it by digesting starches and sugars.

**Dehydrating**

If you're looking for ways to store food that is not dependent on refrigeration, dehydration is a great way. Dehydrated foods pack all the nutritional punch of fresh foods without space commitment and stringent storage parameters. Dehydrated foods that are nutritious while fresh will also be nutritious when dried. All you have to do is add some water and you'll have a meal or at least one component.

# FOOD

Dehydration allows you to preserve the nutritional value of produce by removing all water from the food. With little moisture in the food, you'll be able to then extend its lifespan of it. Without moisture, it's difficult for most bacteria to grow on it, even if the food is not refrigerated. Dehydrated foods may remain fresh for 5–15 years.

Sun-drying food is the most cost-effective method for drying food; just make sure the food is screened off to prevent contamination by insects

Drying food with the sun will require high heat and unfiltered sun. Drying food outside is best done in a screened box designed for drying. The food will need to be placed on screens. It is also necessary to have a frame with a screen in it to keep bugs off your food. There are plans for making one of these contraptions on the internet.

It is a good idea to have a combination of dried, canned, and freeze-dried foods. The latest will store for longer, but unfortunately, you cannot do that process at home. You can, however, successfully can and dry food that will sit on your shelf for years without spoiling.

You must follow the directions for canning. Don't try and cheat the system or cut corners. Vegetables and meat absolutely must be preserved in a pressure canner. Fruits are easier and can be processed in a boiling water bath or basically a stockpot on the stove.

Fruit should be washed and dried. If the fruit's skin is not edible, one should peel the fruit.

Remove any fruit seeds before cutting them into half an inch cubes and coating them in fresh lemon juice. Place the fruit slices in a single layer on the racks of the dehydrator or on baking pans coated with parchment paper. Dehydrate in a dehydrator for six to eight hours at 135 degrees Fahrenheit until the food is dry and crisp. Alternately, one may bake the fruit slices in an oven preheated to 200 degrees Fahrenheit for two to three hours, turning them over once throughout the baking process until the chips are crisp. Keep all dried fruit in a cold, dry, and dark area, sealed tightly in an airtight container.

## Methods of Dehydration

Dehydration can be achieved in several ways: air drying, sun drying, oven drying, food dehydrators, or even in smokehouses. The method you choose is entirely based on the resources available to you and your preference.

### Air Drying

Hanging foods indoors to dry in the air is an example of air drying. This requires adequate airflow and the protection of foods from dirt and insects. Keep in mind that this only works in low-humidity areas, or else the food will mold before it dries.

### Drying in the Sun

Sun drying is the most traditional method of drying. If you live somewhere with plenty of sunlight, it is completely free. However, because it is dependent on the weather, it cannot be accurately planned for.

Food usually takes three or four days to dry in the sun, and mold will grow if it doesn't dry in that time. For three to five days, the sky should be clear, and the temperature should be 95°F or higher, with less than 20% humidity. This method is not for you if you cannot guarantee all of these conditions.

### Drying in the Oven

Food can be easily dried in the oven. It may take six or more hours to properly dry food. These foods will require low heat to dry effectively, and some may only require a gas pilot light. If possible, set your oven to 140°F and leave the door ajar to allow for circulation. However, due to the length of time required, this method is very expensive. You could also burn food by accident.

### Dehydrators for Food

Food dehydrators use a heating element, fans, and vents to heat and circulate air to dry foods. Dried foods shrink and become lighter, and a good dehydrator retains more flavor and color. These typically enable more food to be dried faster, more consistently, and sometimes more efficiently. These devices, however, take up counter space and can be costly if you choose one with all the bells and whistles.

Drying Foods, particularly meats, can be dried in a smoker. This not only dries out the food but also adds a nice smoky flavor. This usually necessitates a temperature of 145°-150°F, as well as plenty of smoke to dry out the food. Depending on the food, this can take anywhere from 12 to 72 hours.

### What Not to Dehydrate

Some foods that may be available commercially in dried forms are not safe to dry at home for safety reasons. In particular, you want to avoid dehydrating butter, cheese, eggs, or milk. It's too easy to do so poorly or cause spoilage. However, dried eggs, cheese, butter, and milk should definitely be purchased as part of your stockpile.

### Canning

Canning is only one of the ways you can preserve the excess from your garden. Drying or dehydrating fruits, vegetables, and meats is another option. Drying is a bit more time-consuming, but it is much lighter and space-friendly than canning. If you are storing food in your car or a bug-out bag, dried food is always better than canned food.

Dried food can be eaten as is, think jerky or trail mix, or reconstituted to bring the food reasonably close to its original state. One of the downsides to drying or dehydrating your food is the fact that you lose some of the nutritional value in the process. The vitamins and minerals tend to be in the juice for fruits and veggies.

It is a good idea to learn how to do your own home canning and drying food so you can do it post-collapse. It is a skill you can pass down to your children as well. Fifty years ago, canning food was the norm in households. We have gotten away from home preservation in the past couple of decades. The reasons why vary, but basically, we are too busy and would rather the convenience of commercially prepared foods over the effort it takes to take care of the job at home.

When you are ready with all of the essentials required for canning, you can just heat the sealed and filled jars, which causes your food to undergo expansion, give up steam and push the air out of the jars. When you cool it down, this will then form a vacuum seal over the jar. Hence, this executes the process of canning! Some of the factors that affect the canning process and its shelf-life are its acidity and sugar content. Therefore, it is better to follow the canning recipe for specific items to get a good start at first.

Two home canning methods are preferable on priority such as water bath canning and pressure canning. Water bath canning is the lower-temperature canning method. It is accountable for only the high-acid recipes or foods with an ideal measure of acid content. There is a recommendation for jams, fruits, salsa, jellies, pickles, tomatoes, sauces, pie fillings, condiments, chutneys, or sauces.

On the other hand, pressure canning is a high-temperature process that is accountable for safely preserving low-acidic foods or recipes. This home canning method is recommended for poultry, meats, chili, vegetables, seafood, and others. But you should remember not to use a pressure cooker for this canning process, as the models vary from one another, which might trigger a change in results.

Canning of food preserves all of the nutrients of your food or recipe. You just need to follow the ideal process of executing the canning steps. Depending upon that fact, you will always be able to preserve your recipes or foods for your prepper pantry and survival needs.

**What do you need for Canning?**

Canning might seem a complex process by its name, but the steps are pretty much easy for you to adapt. There are some things that you should have to adapt to this process. They include:

- **Jar Filter Tongs**—The tongs are useful for picking up the hot jars and taking them out of the hot water bath or pressure chamber after processing.
- **Ladle**—The ladle is used for spooning the food into their respective canning jars.
- **Canning Jars and Seals**—You need to use glass mason jars with sealed lids as your canning containers.
- **Wide-Mouth Funnel**—The wider-mouth funnel will come with a large opening for fitting the jars. Hence, this makes it easy for you to fill jars and keep their rims clean.
- **Large Pot/Water-Bath Canner**—If you intend to focus on canning jams, fruits, pickles, salsa, jellies, or others, a large pot or water-bath canner will serve the purpose. You can use the pressure canning method at high temperatures for canning vegetables, meat, seafood, poultry, etc.

Hence, this is all about canning and its importance in preserving foods for prepping emergency pantries. When you know that there is a scope for preparing your food and preserving it for a long-term emergency survival need, you will eventually be able to save a lot of money on it. Therefore, it is an important process for the preppers to adapt!

**Freezing**

Freezing is an effective method of food preservation. It kills bacteria on almost any food, making it safe to eat. Aside from that, it's also quite simple. All you need to do is store foods in a cool place for a period of time and expect them to be edible when you return.

On that note, since the invention of solar-powered refrigerators, freezing is a food preservation method that people who want to live off-the-grid should not overlook. You can build your own fridge or purchase one. Although a purchase will cost at least $1,000, it is cost-effective. It will be especially useful if you intend to live off the grid for several years.

Except for eggs in their shell, almost all foods can be frozen raw after blanching and/or cooking. So, the real question here is which foods do not freeze well. The following foods are generally not suitable for freezing:

Cream sauces separate even when completely warmed after being frozen.

Mayonnaise, cream cheese, and cottage cheese don't hold up well, and their textural quality suffers as a result.

Milk appears to be a 50-50 bet. While it can be safely frozen, it occasionally separates after freezing. When mixed, this milk can be used for cooking and baking.

Precooked meat can be frozen, but it lacks the moisture of raw meat and will frequently dry out if frozen for more than four weeks.

**Facts about Frosty**

When it comes to freezing, the magic number is zero. Microbes go dormant at 0°F. The food will not spoil, and any germs will not breed until it is defrosted. However, keep in mind that the longer the food is frozen, the more it loses certain qualities, such as vivid flavor and texture. Always freeze things at their peak, and remember that cooking defrosted food as soon as it's thawed will also stop microbial growth.

The first step in freezing is to keep the items cold until you're ready to use them. This is especially important with meat, but it also affects how fruits and vegetables come out of the freezer.

**Notes:** Using fresh snow or iced water from a lake, pond, sea, or any nearby water source is an option.

Frozen food temperatures must not exceed 30°C.

Wrapping frozen foods in sawdust or wool causes the melting process to take longer.

With your decision to live off-the-grid comes the need to learn about other food preservation techniques. Since you'll be stationed somewhere that may be far from convenience stores, fast food chains, restaurants, and other dining places, have fun as you rely on your own resources.

**Other Food Preservation Techniques**

- **Curing**—food preservation technique that involves soaking products in a solution that contains nitrites or salt and water.
- **Dry Salting**—a food preservation technique ideal for all types of meat and fruits and vegetables.
- **Fermenting**—a food preservation technique that is meant to promote good bacterial growth.

## FOOD

- **Smoke Drying**—a food preservation technique ideal for preserving fish and other types of meat. The idea behind it is to terminate pests that may surround the raw products.
- **Sun Drying**—a food preservation technique ideal for preserving fish and other types of meat. It is also used for fruits and vegetables. The idea behind it is to terminate the bacteria that are likely to be growing on wet surfaces with the sun's heat.

**Using yeast to preserve food and learn how to ferment vegetables:** Two garlicky cloves should be placed at the base of a quart-sized clear glass jar. Three cups of diced vegetables, such as carrots, cauliflower, green beans, or cabbage, should be stacked in the jar with between one and three inches of headroom between each layer.

**How to preserve vanilla beans in alcohol and make oner own homemade vanilla:** Five whole vanilla seeds should be divided in half to use a lengthwise incision. Place the peas in an eight-ounce container and top them with vodka, covering them completely. Shake it to combine the ingredients after covering it. It should be stored somewhere dark and cool for a minimum of 2 months. The longer the vanilla is allowed to stand, the stronger its flavor will get.

**Preserving fish using sugar and salt:** Prepare one 2-pound piece of salmon by drying and washing it (or other fish like mackerel, tuna, cod, or trout). Each cup of glucose and one-half teacup of kosher salt should be combined in a medium dish before being combined with one-half cup of raw dill leaves and applied to the fish all over. Put it in a shallow glass dish and weigh it down with such a heavy pot after having it well covered in many layers of plastic wrap. On the first day, flip it over once and let it rest in the refrigerator for two to three days. In the refrigerator, cured fish may be stored for up to 3 days.

**Preserving food in vinegar:** In a bowl, combine 12 cups of rice vinegar, 1 tablespoon of sugar, and 2 teaspoons of salt by whisking the ingredients together. Add half a cup of thinly sliced veggies, such as cucumbers, carrots, or red onion, and let them set out at room temperature for half an hour.

**Preserve sun-dried tomatoes in olive oil:** To rehydrate half a cup of sun-dried tomatoes, place them in a big saucepan and add two cups of boiling water and two cups of red wine vinegar. It should take between five and ten minutes for the tomatoes to become ripe and plump once the mixture has been allowed to simmer over low heat. After removing the pan from the heat and allowing it to cool for a further five minutes, drain the liquid from the pan and pat it dry with paper towels. Place the tomatoes in a glass jar, add one teaspoon of dried oregano and a sprinkle of chili flakes, and then fill the container with olive oil, making sure that the tomatoes are thoroughly submerged in the oil. Keep for up to three months in the refrigerator after opening.

# CHAPTER 3: TYPES OF CEREALS FOR STORAGE

### Delicate Grains

Things like corn meal, grain, quinoa, and rye offer undeniably more than making a delectable breakfast. They additionally give as long as eight years of food-safe storage when appropriately fixed.

It is basic that oxygen safeguards are added to the containers and fixed; in any case, they are probably going to spoil. Commonly, it's ideal to buy delicate grains in a sealed shut compartment from the maker straightforwardly.

# PREPPER'S LONG-TERM SURVIVAL GUIDE

**Hard Grains**

Hard grains, like white wheat, millet, and buckwheat, are one more grain to look out for. They can be utilized for a grouping of easy-to-understand recipes immediately. Not at all like delicate grains, hard grains can endure significantly longer (as long as 12 years) with legitimate storage.

**Dry Pasta**

A thrilling element of dry pasta is that it can possibly endure significantly longer than you'd naturally suspect, particularly if you're somebody who commonly goes by the best-before dates on bundling.

Most sorts of dry pasta at your nearby merchant will endure as long as two years past its expiry date, making it a brilliant choice for making consoling dinners when there's no other option. By and large, pasta can endure as long as 30 years, which is comparable to beans and rice, mainly if it's kept in an impermeable holder. Think about a few assortments, including entire wheat pasta.

**Flour**

During a highly sensitive situation or a cataclysmic event, one of the primary things that take off your supermarket's racks is flour, basically because it's one of the most multi-reason fixings that is likewise reasonable.

Luckily, flour has a wonderful timeframe of realistic usability of as long as 25 years, for however long it is unground. Preferably, you will need to have the proper hardware to ground the flour on an on-request premise, guaranteeing it has its greatest period of usability.

You will likewise need to ensure that it is stored in a fixed bundle with an oxygen safeguard.

**Beans**

If you would prefer to zero in fundamentally on canned foods for a medium-term storage arrangement, canned beans can be an extraordinary option compared to dried ones. You can anticipate that most canned beans should endure as long as six years for however long they are stored in a cool and dry spot. Quite possibly, the main thing while canning foods is to think about botulism, as it very well may be destructive.

## CHAPTER 4: THE ART OF GETTING BY

**A Guide to Identifying, Collecting and Preparing Wild Edible Plants**

Wild edibles can be found virtually anywhere. Foraging helped early humans survive, so it can help us in an emergency situation.

There are various berries to be found in the wild, but you cannot simply pluck and eat them all. If you don't know which berries to eat, at the very least, you should know which ones to avoid! You should avoid the berries of plants such as holly, yew, dogwood, and pokeweed. You can eat gooseberries, mulberries, muscadine, elderberries, and other berries.

There should be several courses available on foraging for wild edibles. Local classes are great because they teach you about edibles that you might find in your area. It is also critical to understand which types of plants are found during which seasons. Going for walks or hiking and practicing identifying plants is a great way to become acquainted with the edibles in your area. You must keep

## FOOD

in mind that some of the berries and plants you come across can be dangerous, and eating them can have serious health consequences. It is therefore critical to understand which are safe to eat and which are not. Eating dangerous plants will only make matters worse.

Don't rely solely on outward signs of identification. Several edible wild plants appear to be very similar to one another. Determine how to distinguish between plants of the same species based on their smell, touch, and other characteristics. Toxic plants, while not always the case, frequently have an unpleasant taste and odor. However, this is not a hard and fast rule. However, one should only use one taste if one is absolutely certain that the plant is not harmful. Certain plants, such as water hemlock, can be lethal even at low concentrations. Learn about habitat: Learn about plants that grow people together. Some plants grow in close proximity to others, which is not uncommon. There is a good chance that if one finds a yellow dock, one will also find people in the surrounding area. Acquire the knowledge and skills needed to locate wild plants that can be used for food all year. This is significant for several reasons. The first step is to positively identify the item. Another reason to keep track of wild edible plants all year is to identify perennial plants that can be harvested at the start of the growing season. For example, by the time people can be recognized, it is frequently too late to use it effectively. If you make a mental note of where it is while it is still visible during the warmer months, you will be ready to spot it when it reappears in the spring.

Elderberries, for example, are acceptable to consume after they have been cooked, but the plant's bark, stems, and roots are believed to be toxic. It is also essential to keep in mind that specific

periods of the year are the only times when particular plants may be consumed. For instance, one shouldn't use stinging nettle after it has produced seeds since it loses its medicinal value.

# PREPPER'S LONG-TERM SURVIVAL GUIDE

## Growing Your Own Food Is an Environmentally Sustainable Way to Produce Food

Our gardens can provide us with great food sources and we should take full advantage of them. Growing food takes time and, in an emergency, it will certainly be hard to acquire any seeds from the store, so it is best to be prepared.

But in times of peace, the store is the best place to find seeds for growing vegetables, in fact, you can also harvest the seeds from the fruits and vegetables that you grow in order to grow more.

Planning how to grow food is a time-consuming process, however, it is essential if you want to have access to an array of different fruits and vegetables. You can start by listing the vegetables that you and your family usually eat. Then, you will need to understand what type of crops grow well in the area you live in, as well as the times it takes to grow each crop and how to grow them properly. You should stock up on those seeds and if you can, you should start growing your little garden straight away and not wait for it to be too late. Having the necessary experience in an emergency situation can be extremely helpful.

There are many environmental benefits of growing your own food. For one, you'll reduce the amount of energy required to transport food. By eliminating the need for transportation, you'll also minimize the carbon footprint associated with food production. Also, your produce will travel much shorter distances, cutting down on the use of packaging and pesticides. Not only will you be doing your part to help protect our planet, but you'll also benefit from reduced amounts of salmonella strains and packaging.

Produce from your own garden is fresher and more nutritious. Purchasing it at the store has an incredibly long transportation time, impacting freshness and taste. Plus, your produce has probably been sitting on a shelf for a long time, losing nutrients as it travels. Not to mention all of the energy and waste associated with transportation. And while we can't change our habits overnight, we can try to make a difference in the way we eat.

Another environmental benefit of growing your own food is lowering your grocery bill. You'll save money by not buying produce from supermarkets. Additionally, you'll be reducing your reliance on the pollinating industry. By buying organic produce, you can avoid the negative impacts of monocropping and other farming practices. You can even preserve your own seeds and feed your family year-round. All of these benefits are worth a try.

Another benefit of growing your own food is the opportunity to teach your children about weather and environmental factors. Your children will gain valuable knowledge about environmental issues and enjoy growing their own food. It will also become a family project and a fun way to teach children about the importance of sustainability and eating healthy food. It may even inspire a lifelong passion for food! The possibilities are endless. So, start growing your own food today.

## Raising Animals

You should also consider raising animals as having a diverse diet is very important, even more so in an emergency situation. Things like chickens, rabbits, sheep, and goats are easier to get and take care of. Many online and offline classes can teach you how to raise farm animals, but you should opt for offline courses as you will probably get more practical experience that way.

If you want something other than meat and have the space, consider raising tilapia fish. These fish are simple to breed and grow quickly; all you need is a small pond and food.

# FOOD

While living off the grid is legal in some countries, you must be fully self-sufficient in terms of food production before you do so. Raising livestock is a component of this. A couple of goats, sheep, chickens, geese, or cows, for example, can go a long way toward providing meat, eggs, and milk for domestic consumption if the laws allow.

## Livestock Production Requires Permits

To begin, you should be aware that each country has laws and regulations in place to keep order in areas where off-grid living is permitted. For example, city and county ordinances, as well as zoning restrictions, limit certain off-grid lifestyles. Certain activities on your property are prohibited by these restrictions.

When it comes to animal husbandry, you should check your city or county zoning regulations to see what you can and cannot do on your property. Almost every city and county has breed and number restrictions on the animals you can keep. The laws are not universal because they differ by country. Instead of making assumptions, researching the laws in your city is the best way to learn what is permitted. The laws governing livestock rearing on off-grid properties can be found in various sections of city and county codes. Similarly, before beginning your project, you must first consult with the appropriate authorities.

You can proceed with caution if the laws do not expressly prohibit something. The following are some examples of common types of laws to be wary of.

- Sanitation and health
- Zoning regulations and permitted uses
- Nuisance legislation
- Noise regulations

Check your city or county laws regarding the keeping of various animals on your property. In most cases, county zoning is the most important factor in livestock raising. There may be no strict regulations if you live in the country.

## What Kinds of Animals Can You Raise on an Off-Grid Property?

When you are familiar with your county's livestock laws, the next step is to select self-sufficient animals. If you have suitable land, these are simple to keep and do not require any additional feed. There are numerous animal species to consider. Before you begin, keep in mind that purchasing too many animals at once can be a recipe for disaster. The following are some of the most beneficial and productive animals to consider.

### Chickens

Chickens are by far the most popular and ideal homestead livestock for your project. If you want to move to self-sufficiency, both new and experienced homesteaders can find comfort in poultry projects. Your hens will provide you with fresh eggs, eliminating the need for you to visit the nearest grocery store. You can get meat from your roosters as well. One advantage of chickens is that they can be processed without the assistance of another person.

Chickens are also useful for pest control around the homestead. Instead of using pesticides to control bugs and insects, let your chickens do it for you. Chickens also make gardening easier because their constant scratching loosens the soil. More importantly, hens will add manure to the soil, increasing its fertility, which is beneficial to crop production.

Another advantage of chickens is that, depending on the breed, they are a low-cost investment. Commercial bird varieties can mature in eight to twelve weeks. Egg-laying birds begin laying eggs after six months and can lay eggs for up to two years. Dual-purpose breeds that can be kept for meat and eggs are disease resistant and self-sufficient in terms of food. Meat from egg-laying chickens has an excellent flavor but is not very tender. The birds can be harvested early for meat.

To maximize chicken productivity, construct a secure shelter to protect them from predators and the elements. To avoid disease outbreaks, keep the number of birds under control. Chickens are simple to care for because most breeds are hardy and can live on their own. Overall, keeping chickens has no disadvantages as long as proper procedures are followed.

**Goats**

Goats are a good option if you want to progress to larger animals. There are several advantages to raising goats on your farm. These are hardy creatures that require little upkeep. There are no other costs to consider aside from the initial cost of purchasing your goats. Goats are grazers and are simple to manage because they do not require supplemental feeding. They can survive in a variety of climates with little care.

Goats are small and can be housed in a small space. All you need to do is construct a proper shed to protect your goats from the elements. These animals can remove unwanted plants and produce manure for your garden. They are effective at removing invasive plants from your property. Goats will also warn you if something is wrong so that you can take the necessary action.

Moreover, goats provide milk and meat. They are the most basic livestock to begin with if you want milk and meat. They also breed quickly, which means you'll have a steady supply of milk and meat. Goat milk is delicious and adds a rich flavor to tea or coffee. There is no special equipment required to milk or slaughter goats for meat. You should, however, check your local laws regarding the slaughter of livestock.

**Pigs**

Pigs provide meat and fat, which can be used for a variety of purposes on the farm. These animals are extremely efficient at converting waste into high-quality meat. When you keep pigs, you won't have to worry about dealing with waste food and garden scraps because they provide good feed for your livestock. If you let them roam around your property, they can also clear the land for gardening purposes. Swine can eat almost anything, making them economical.

Pigs, on the other hand, are not appropriate for suburban settings. Make sure you are serious about raising these animals if you live in the county. You must clean them on a regular basis, which can be difficult. The boars provide highly potent manure that can boost garden productivity. You can make your own bacon, sausages, and ham with porkers. These are special foods that you should keep on hand for special occasions. You can slaughter your piglet if you have the right tools and skills.

Bees are an excellent addition to any homestead. Keeping a beehive on your property may appear frightening at first, but you will soon realize that domestic bees are calm. People who have kept bees before can handle them without wearing protective equipment. Bees are not dangerous if they are not provoked.

Keeping bees has several advantages. Once you have the necessary equipment, such as beehives, bees require very little to no maintenance. Because honey is made from natural ingredients, you don't need to buy any feed for your bees. There is no need for you to do any maintenance on your bees.

Bee honey can also be used as a source of sugar in your self-sufficient household. Honey has medicinal properties and is extremely beneficial to your health and immune system. When you live in a remote location, you may not have regular access to healthcare. As a result, you must have a strong immune system to deal with ailments such as fever, flu, and others without resorting to medication. Bees can also play an important role in plant pollination, which leads to increased crop productivity in your plot. Furthermore, bees play an important role in assisting fruit trees to produce healthy fruits. The population of wild bees is declining in many areas, and keeping beehives is an excellent way to help increase their numbers.

**Cows**

A cow is a fantastic source of milk and meat. If you're serious about long-term food and milk production, you should consider raising a few cows. Check your county's zoning laws first to determine the number of cows permitted on your property. The main advantage of keeping a cow is that it can be pastured on grass for the majority of the year. If you have a lot of pasture land, cows can be a good investment. This is not possible, however, because country homesteads have acreage restrictions. During the winter, you may require additional stock feed.

Cows produce manure, which is beneficial to the garden. You can make organic plant food out of cow manure without using any artificial fertilizers. When you decide to raise a couple of cows at your off-grid home, you must make an informed decision. To keep the cattle from straying, you'll need a barn and tall fences. If you keep dairy cows, however, you may require milking equipment. One cow can produce up to 20 liters of milk; milking them with your hands can be difficult. Furthermore, because milk spoils quickly, you may require adequate storage equipment. If you manage your small dairy project carefully, you may be able to supply milk to people in your county.

**Sheep**

You can keep sheep at your homestead if you stay in the northern region. Sheep are naturally adapted to colder climates and live on pasture. These animals can clear bushes around your property and provide manure to help plants grow. Sheep, like goats, are small and docile, making them easy to manage.

Sheep can be a good source of income if properly managed. This is an excellent animal that produces both milk and meat. Sheep meat and other products, such as cheese, are rare and in high demand in various parts of the world. You can make a lot of money selling organic products made locally to restaurants and farmers' markets. Apart from providing meat and milk for family consumption, these animals can be profitable if their wool is harvested. Knitters can spend a lot of money on wool, which is in high demand due to its high quality. You can combine wool with fibers from other animals, such as mohair goats, angora rabbits, or alpacas.

The disadvantage of keeping sheep is that they require special care and are a favorite prey item for many predators. You must care for them full-time because they are very docile and you may not know if they are being attacked. If you are a new sheep keeper, you may not know what they require because they can die for no apparent reason. The animals are generally good, but their upkeep can be difficult.

### Geese

Geese are good birds to keep at your homestead because they can protect other animals. They usually sound an alarm to warn you of an intruder or to frighten away predators. Geese are also aggressive and effective fighters. They are just as good as dogs and will provide you with peace of mind if you live in a remote off-grid home.

Another advantage of keeping geese is that they produce large eggs and meat, both of which are delectable. They outperform turkey meat and other large species of birds. Goose meat, like turkey, is typically reserved for special holiday feasts. This distinguishes the geese and makes them potentially profitable if their eggs and meat are sold.

### Ducks

Ducks are useful birds to consider for your off-grid homestead. If you have a slug problem in your garden, you can keep ducks to keep them away. Ducks are uncommon, so you can mix them in with other types of fowl you have at home. These creatures are lovely to watch as they swim around in the pond.

Ducks produce delicious meat and eggs, making them suitable for sale to some fine dining establishments. Duck meat is scarce, so you can charge a premium for it. When keeping ducks, you should put health and sanitation first. To prevent disease outbreaks, ensure that the pond has clean water. Protect the ducks from predators that could harm them.

### Rabbits

Rabbits, like chickens, are essential to include on your homestead animal list. Rabbits provide delicious, lean, and healthy meat. The high-quality meat is easily digestible and nutrient-dense. Butchering and processing a rabbit are a breeze. Processing the meat does not require any special equipment. You can also sell the meat for a profit if you want.

Rabbits produce excellent manure, which can be used directly without the need for composting. When the rabbits produce excess manure, you can sell it to other people to generate revenue. While we're on the subject of composting and manure production, rabbits can eat green grass and other materials that you don't need. They also consume garden scraps, making it easier to break down the material when it is added to compost.

Rabbits produce fiber and pelts that can be used in crafts. You can raise rabbits to meet your needs if you enjoy hobbies such as knitting or other crafts. You can make some money by selling extra fiber. Another advantage of keeping rabbits is that they are legal in most areas, so you won't have to worry about zoning regulations in your county. They can easily grow in any environment as long as a comfortable shelter is provided. Look for a safe cage that will keep the rabbits safe from dogs and other predators. You can become a very successful rabbit farmer with very little space.

Rabbits are docile, making them ideal for young children. Rabbits are an excellent way to introduce your children to livestock rearing. The animals are very easy to handle and pose no threat to the handler. However, because rabbits are cute, some people may be tempted to keep them as pets.

### Fish

While fish are not considered animals, they have a long history in agriculture. You can add fish to your self-sufficient homestead to get a consistent source of protein. Fish are simple to care for and multiply quickly, even on a small scale. Another advantage of keeping fish is that they are permitted

# FOOD

almost everywhere, so no license is required. Fish make no noise that can disturb your peace of mind at home.

Fish also produce a lot of fertilizer, which you can use to fertilize your garden. If you're feeling daring, you can build a permaculture duck pond and channel the water into your garden via a drainage system. If used correctly, this method can be extremely productive. Alternatively, you can add fish fertilizer to the hydroponic system. This will directly fertilize the plants, promoting effective growth. Fish do not leave a mess and pose no risk of escaping, which distinguishes them from other livestock. In addition to providing meat, fish can improve the quality of the ecosystem around your home.

### Quail

These are small birds that you can keep on your farm to produce eggs and meat. The meat produced by these birds is exotic and can command high market prices. Quail birds, regardless of size, can generate a lot of money. Specialty creatures like these birds require little space and can be sold to some fine dining establishments. In terms of maintenance, the birds are not overly demanding.

### Worms

Worms, as previously stated, play an important role in improving soil texture and quality. They create "vermicompost," which is valuable compost that improves soil fertility. They can also be used as fish bait when you go fishing. You can sell this high-quality compost for a profit or use it in your garden for maximum productivity. If you want to keep worms, you can get started quickly. Worms multiply quickly if the ground is kept moist. To feed the worms, you should also add biodegradable materials such as plant waste and manure.

As you have observed, you can keep different types of animals at your off-grid homestead to ensure that you are fully self-sufficient. It is crucial to do some research to gain insight into the permitted animals on the homestead. When choosing domestic animals, as a novice, get the ones that are easy to keep to achieve maximum sustainability when you live off-grid. You also need to understand the best ways to use livestock products like meat, milk, wool, and eggs. You should master the skill of slaughtering animals and other methods of different harvesting products.

### Fishing, Hunting, and Trapping

### Go for the Creepy Crawling Critters

If you are running short on food and in desperate need of food, you might have to eat the little critters you will find crawling on the ground. They often hide beneath certain things. The best thing is that most of these critters are great protein sources, and very few of them are poisonous. But this rule of finding food has certain exceptions, which are defined in terms of guidelines for you to decide on the edibility of bugs:

Stay away from the bugs that have bright colors. This rule is accountable for most creatures and not just bugs or insects. It is said that the most deadly creatures often look the most beautiful.

If the smell of the bug is bad, you must let it go and not even taste it. The only identified exception to this rule is the stink bug, which smells bad but is edible. To be on the safe side, ignore them all! The bugs that are hairy and prefer to sting/bite should be avoided at all costs. If you do not have direct knowledge of how to process such insects or bugs for eating, it is better to avoid taking risks with them.

Caterpillars, tomato worms, and black ants are good protein sources and are edible. The tarantulas

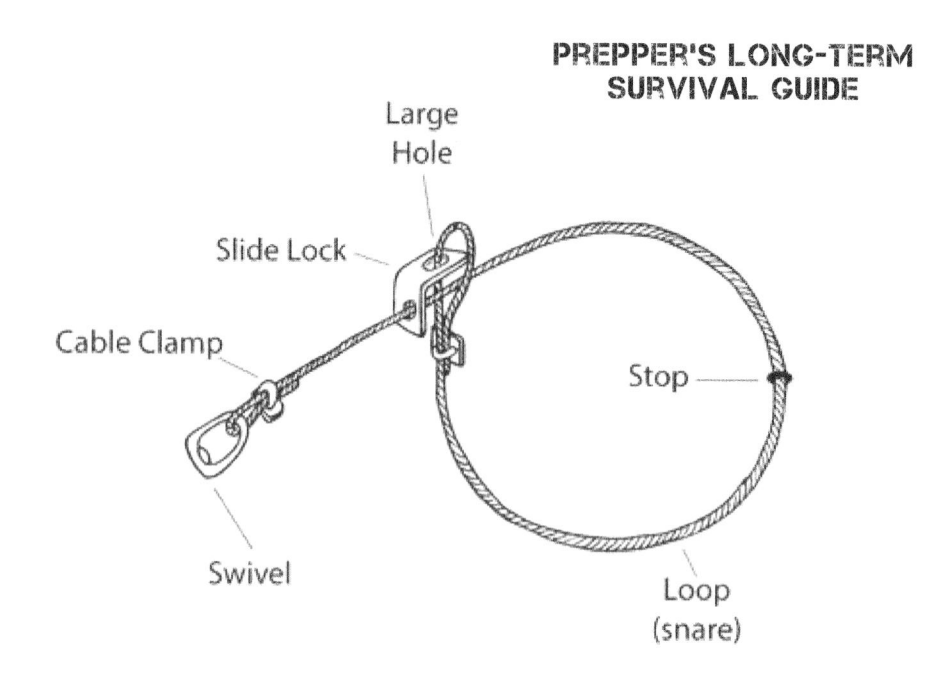

*Diagram of a snare with labeled parts: Large Hole, Slide Lock, Cable Clamp, Swivel, Stop, Loop (snare)*

and scorpions are also good protein sources and are edible if they are cooked well.

**Fishing**

When fishing for survival, automatic fishing reels and trotlines can help you increase your catches. A trotline is a heavy line that has smaller ones hanging from it, allowing you to have more lines in the water and, thus a greater chance of capturing more fish. It is easier to fish using trotlines in rivers and smaller streams where water runs rather than in more static waters such as lakes. A rope, or a larger cord, is placed across a river's banks, and in between those, you have smaller threads of fish lines called snoods. Because each snood has a hook, the odds of success increase exponentially. There are a few things that you need to know when fishing with trotlines, such as the precise space between snoods. You need to leave space between the smaller lines to stop them from tangling. Another great advantage of fishing with a trotline is that you don't necessarily need to be holding the rod, you can leave it and come back and check it a few times a day to retrieve fish and to free more hooks. However, this might not be the best option if you don't have the river or the stream to yourself, as other people might come and steal your hard-caught fish.

With automatic reels, you have more freedom to do other things while you are fishing. You will find them in most fishing and hunting shops, and they will certainly be of great help if you find yourself in survival mode. All you need to do is drop the hook with the bait into the water and attach the reel to something heavy like a tree trunk or a rock. When hooked, the fish's struggling will activate the reel to pull out of the water and retract the line.

But of course, it is not as simple as finding a river and going fishing. You need to know where to fish and if the fish population around your area is healthy enough to keep producing fish for the long term. Knowing the species that live in the lake or river will also help you find the best way to capture the fish.

# FOOD

## Trapping

Traps are a great way to acquire wild meat, mainly because you won't need to be present at all times, you just need to set up the trap and come and check on it once in a while to see if you have caught something. In fact, if this is going to be your way of obtaining wild meat, you should set quite a few and check them at least once every day. However, you don't want to spend too much time in the same place setting up traps or constantly checking if they have caught anything, as this might frighten the very creatures you want to capture.

There are many varieties of snares and other traps that are easy to set up. However, understanding how to properly use a snare, takes some practice. It is good to understand what type of animals you can trap in your area, so you can set up the right size of snares and know where to place them.

## What is a Snare Trap?

Snares are an excellent tool for catching small wildlife. It is known that early civilizations exploited these traps as a way of survival. These traps are now utilized by hunters, fur trappers, survivalists, and indigenous people in a more updated version. Snares are portable and lightweight.

How to set up a snare?

1) Anchor your snare

Anchoring your snare is the easiest step. Make a loop through the swivel using 550 cord, multipurpose wire, or even a wire coat hanger. After that, tie it firmly around the trunk of a tree or other sturdy object.

2) Setting your snare

Snares work best near tiny, well-traveled pathways. "Runs" are a common name for these trails. These runs frequently lead to places with water, cover, nests, and dens.

Once you anchor your snare, adjust the head height for your target animal. Make sure you put the loop in an area where it can support itself up.

Remember if the snare is too high up, the targeted animal will crawl right under it.

- Raccoon - Loop size: 8"- 9" Snare height: 3" to 4"
- Beaver - Loop size 9" -10"   Snare height 2" to 3"
- Bobcat - Loop size 7" - 8"    Snare height: 10" to 12"
- Coyote - Loop size 9" - 10"  Snare height 9" to 10"
- Rabbit -  Loop size 3" - 4.5" Snare height 1.5" to 2.5"

## Hunting

Your ability to hunt for wild meat really depends on your skill and experience. Usually, people hunt using firearms or bows. You need to know the population of wild animals in your area and what species live there. If it is mainly a big game, such as deer, you might be better off by hunting, however, if the local wildlife population is more based on smaller animals such as rabbits or foxes, then trapping might be easier for you to put food on the table.

Many creatures live in the frigid wilderness, and you should be able to capture some of them with the help of a few bear traps. It's best to ensure you can start a fire before placing traps; this is the safest way to eat animal meat. Of course, if you're starving and don't have any other options, raw meat will have to suffice.

A simple noose is the easiest trap to set. Animal tracks might help you decide where to set this trap. The prints will be quite visible if it is genuinely snowing, and even if the ground is frozen, the trail they take through the forest should be visible. From the size of the prints, it left and the amount of harm it causes as it goes through the undergrowth, you should be able to estimate the animal's size. If you follow the footprints, you'll most likely find a common feeding place or a watering spot for the animals. This is a great spot to set up your snares because the more animals in an area, the better your chances of trapping one.

Make a loop and a knot with some of the rope you have on hand, potentially from your Para cord bracelet, to allow you to tighten the noose. The slack end of the rope should then be firmly tied to a solid object, such as a stout tree. Place a stick in the path to keep the noose section in the air and out of the way of the animal. This relieves the rope's tension; without the stick, the noose will tighten on its own. The concept is straightforward: the animal goes into the noose, & the stick springs free. The noose tightens, the more the animal resists. Position several of these around the feeding site to boost your chances of capturing something.

**Cooking Off-the-Grid**

The new age of convenience and technology has overlooked cooking as a necessary survival skill. Fresh-grown produce and local meats are more available than ever, but the question remains on how to properly store them without resorting to canning or smoking everything. And if you're caught out in the wild, will you know how to start a fire?

**Building a Fire**

Once you have found shelter, build yourself a fire. Fire can be used for warmth, light, cooking, and protection. It is the most essential step in any survival scenario.

To build a fire, you will need three basic things:
- **Tinder**: Small, dry flammable material used to catch a spark and start a fire.
- **Kindling**: Slightly larger but still flammable material that will catch the flame from the tinder and spread it further until it is a bonfire. The best kindling is dead twigs and branches around the size of your thumb.
- **Fuel**: Larger material, usually hardwood or deadfall, to sustain the fire once it has started.

You will need matches or another heat source, such as flint and steel, to start a fire. Pack them in a tight waterproof container to ensure their longevity if you're using matches. To make a matchstick, tease apart a piece of cattail fibers down until they are fine and fluffy. Then roll the fibers into a tight bundle between your fingers, being careful not to crush them. Roll a thin strand of dry grass around the center of the bundle and tie it off with another piece of grass to hold it in place. Once you have a sufficient amount, strike your heat source along the side of the bundle, and it should light immediately.

Once you have a flame, add kindling carefully. You'll notice that smaller pieces of wood will catch easier than larger ones, so focus on placing your kindling around the edges of the fire to begin. As soon as you've got a nice medium-sized flame, add larger wood pieces.

# FOOD

## Cooking Equipment

Now that we've got a flame, we need to cook. Cooking is an essential step in making your food safe to eat, and it also breaks down proteins in the meat, making them easier to digest. This section deals with the actual cookware and utensils needed for cooking.

- **Knife**: A good, sharp knife can be used to slice meats and vegetables, and it can also be used for self-defense, thus giving it a dual purpose.
- **Spoon**: A strong, simple spoon made from a single piece of wood. This will be used to stir the pot and scoop the food into your mouth.
- **Cup**: Any waterproof cup or container that can hold liquids.
- **Bowl**: Any waterproof container that is deep and wide enough to hold a decent amount of food. A bowl can also double up as a plate to eat your cooked and prepared food.
- **Pots**: Preferably, you will want two pots—one for boiling water and one for cooking the meat and vegetables. Pots are made using cast iron, aluminum, or stainless steel. Cast iron is the strongest but heaviest material, so make sure you have a sturdy fire underneath it if you choose to use it. Aluminum pots are lighter but still durable. Stainless steel is the lightest choice of all three materials but is not as strong as aluminum or as durable as cast iron.
- **Stove**: A stove will make cooking easier and faster, but it is not necessary to have one. It can operate using small twigs, wood chips, or even dried dung as fuel. The most efficient way of lighting your stove is with flint and steel. You will then place them under the pot to fuel the stove.
- **Waterproof Container**: A waterproof container, such as a Nalgene bottle, or a waterproof bag made from plastic or rubber, will be needed to transport fresh drinking water. If your container is not impermeable, you can first line it with a heavy-duty Ziploc bag to keep the inside of the container dry.
- **Fire**: The fire you started at the beginning of this section will now come in handy as a source of heat for boiling water and cooking food. If your fire is not hot enough to cook with, have some strong-burning material nearby so you can transfer the flame over to it after the tinder has caught on.

### Glowing Coals

You'll need to use hot coals for cooking larger pieces of food that require an extended amount of time or greater heat than provided by tinfoil or clay cooking methods. Hot coals are great for cooking any type of meat and vegetables and can be continually added to your fire as needed.

To make them, simply place any dry plants or wood inside of your fire pit once you have some embers glowing. The fire will consume its fuel, slowly becoming hotter and hotter over time. To control the intensity of the heat produced, either douse the fire with water to temporarily extinguish it or move the coals around with a stick to spread them out or concentrate them in one area.

### Off-Grid Cookware

Tin cans are the most widely available form of cookware that can be picked up at any grocery store, but they're not exactly ideal for cooking. Aluminum foil also works well and is great for making campfire dinners like burritos or grilled cheese sandwiches. However, it isn't generally meant to hold boiling water or cook anything other than simple foods.

As always, the best containers for cooking are handmade by you. Using clay or even ordinary mud to make your pots and pans will allow you to have perfectly cooked food every time, allowing you to eat right out of them simultaneously. Eating many meals straight from the pot is a great way to conserve your plate, bowl, and cup.

### Cooking Techniques

Each cooking method requires different equipment, so be sure you know what you need before beginning.

#### Basic Cooking Method: Campfire

Campfires are the easiest and most commonly used means of cooking off-the-grid. With enough practice, nearly any food can be cooked over a fire with some simple tools. Even foods that require special techniques, such as fish and certain vegetables, can be cooked over a campfire.

Foods that require a flat rock to cook on should be wrapped in large green leaves before cooking and placed directly on the hot coals. Food wrapped in leaves will not only add flavor from the smoke but also trap moisture inside, so you don't lose anything from your meal.

Foods that require a stick to cook on can be wrapped in leaves like flat-rock foods but work better when skewered. Food cooked this way should be turned every few minutes to ensure even cooking without burning the outside of your food before it is cooked through. Campfires can also be used for roasting tubers such as carrots and potatoes over the coals, but make sure to turn them every few minutes to prevent burning.

#### Primitive Cooking Method: Spit Roast

A spit roast is an efficient way to cook food over a fire. To use this method, dig a pit about six inches deep and three feet wide in the ground. Once you have made the pit, fill it with hot coals. Make sure that there are no hot coals on the surface of the pit.

Next, you will need to find a green stick that can be used as a spit. This stick should be at least two inches in diameter and eight feet long, so it creates enough space between the food and fire to cook properly. Once you have found your stick, sharpen each end, and make sure it is sturdy by bending it. Finally, place the spit over the fire and use a green leafy branch as a brush to coat your food with oil or fat.

# FOOD

Spit roasting can be used to cook almost anything cooked over a campfire but try to keep foods higher than three inches above the coals, so they do not burn. If your spit is thick enough, you can also cook flat-rock foods over a fire using this method.

### Primitive Cooking Method: Stone Oven

Stone ovens are efficient cooking techniques used by cultures such as the Native Americans for generations. The stone oven is created by digging a pit in the ground and lining it with flat rocks. Once you have laid the bricks, create a fire in the pit and let it burn until it has turned to coals. Your stone oven will now be ready for cooking.

To use your stone oven, lay green leaves over your food, then wrap them in clay or mud and another layer of leaves. Place the food directly on the oven floor and cook until ready.

### Primitive Cooking Method: Dirt Oven

Dirt ovens are created by stacking rocks in a pit to create a small cave-like structure where you will place hot coals. Once the pit is filled with rocks and the fire has burned down to coals, you will need to find green leafy branches that can be used as a cover for your fire.

Next, you will need to find small stones about the size of an egg and lay them across the top of your oven. Once this is done, create a small dome-like structure with your leaves and place hot coals inside. Make sure to cover the hole at the top of your oven with leaves or clay before cooking to create an airtight seal. Your food can now be placed in the pit and cooked until ready.

### Tin-Can Cooking Method: Grill

Tin cans are very versatile and can be used for cooking just about anything, but they do require a specific set of equipment to cook food in them. When using tin cans as grills, the cans should be cut open so they lay flat on your heat sources, such as coals or a campfire. Once the cans are flat, you can use them like any other grill by placing meat on top of the can and cooking it.

Tin cans can also be placed directly on top of hot coals and used to steam food. To do this, simply place the meat or vegetables inside before cooking so they can begin heating. When ready, remove the tin can from the heat and let it cool down for a few minutes before opening it up. Whatever you cook should be perfectly steamed and ready to eat.

Tin cans can also be placed over a flame if a grill or grate isn't available, but make sure to place a few rocks around the base before doing so. This will help protect the bottom of your food from burning by providing a barrier between it and the direct heat. If you're using a campfire, rocks can be gathered ahead of time and placed by your fire while you prepare food.

### Tin-Can Cooking Method: Steam

Steam is the healthiest way to cook vegetables off the grid, even more so than boiling them in water. This method will also work with any metal container you might have, but it requires the most amount of time to prepare before cooking your food.

Simply place your vegetables in a metal container and place them safely over the fire. If you have no way to suspend your vegetables above the coals or flame, then build a small lean-to around them using green wood so the shelter suspends them. Once the fire has burned down and the coals are hot, open up your container and spread out any coals or flames that might be touching it. This will ensure only the bottom of your vegetables is cooked instead of burning them on all sides.

### Clay Cooking Method: Pit Oven

To make a clay oven, you will need smooth clay free of rocks or sand, but if these are all available, they can also be used. The basic idea behind this method is to make a container of sorts for your food to cook in. These containers can be made from leaves, large green branches with the bark stripped off, or even mud left to harden overnight before cooking.

This method is simple enough if you have smooth clay on hand that will not burn when directly exposed to fire. Simply dig a hole, place your food inside once you have a fire started in it, and cover the hole with clay until heated through. The longer you leave it in the hole, the hotter your food will get, so plan accordingly before placing it there.

The pit oven can also be used the same way by filling a container made from green wood or leaves with coals and food, putting a layer of clay over the top to seal it, and placing another container or green wood frame inside so your food is suspended while cooking. This method will provide more even heat for longer periods than simply digging a hole and burying your food wrapped in leaves.

### Modern Cooking Method: Tin Foil

Tinfoil is the quickest and easiest way to make delicious meals in the wild since almost all food can be wrapped in it before cooking. To cook using tin foil, simply wrap your vegetables or meat in a sheet of foil, place them over hot coals, and wait for the heat to distribute evenly throughout your food. If you don't have tin foil, then heavy-duty aluminum foil can also be used and will last longer than standard silver foil.

Tinfoil is also great for cooking eggs without having to worry about them breaking. Simply wrap your eggs in tinfoil along with any spices you like, then place them on the hot coals to cook. This cooking method provides perfectly cooked scrambled eggs that are fun to peel since the foil randomly shapes them.

The most important part about cooking while off-the-grid is to keep it simple and easy. When you're worried about catching food, defending yourself from wildlife, or just trying to get a fire built so you don't freeze to death for the night, complicated recipes aren't going to be your top concern. While off-the-grid, the best dishes take little time to prepare and cook, leaving you more time to focus on other important things.

# BOOK 4: WATER

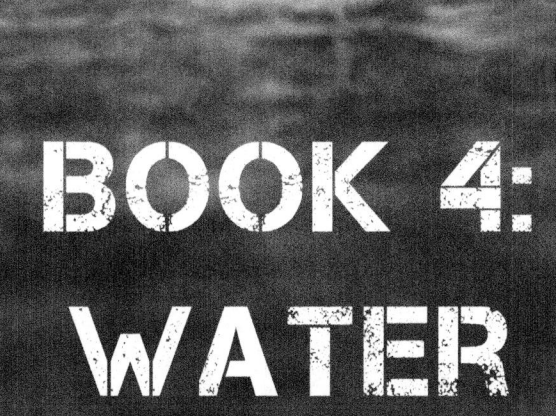

# PREPPER'S LONG-TERM SURVIVAL GUIDE
## CHAPTER 1: THE IMPORTANCE OF WATER

Water is a valuable natural resource that cannot be replaced. It's critical to drink enough water every day, and not just because it makes up roughly 60% of your body. Water also aids in the transport of nutrients into your bloodstream, the detoxification of bodily toxins, the removal of impurities and waste products from your body, and much more. Without water for these purposes, you may experience a variety of health issues that do not manifest themselves in the form of visible symptoms. Hyponatremia (low blood sodium) is a prime example of this, having claimed the lives of numerous athletes during endurance sports such as marathon running. Water is required by the body to perform basic life-sustaining functions such as circulation, digestion, and various biochemical processes. However, we have created a "modern" lifestyle that frequently ignores this fact, resulting in the majority of people not drinking enough water on a daily basis.

Even if you can survive for several days without food in a crisis, your body requires water to function properly. If you don't have access to safe drinking water, you may become dehydrated and develop a variety of medical problems. This could make it difficult for you to defend yourself against looters. During a crisis, having enough safe drinking water available for everyone in your home is critical. As a result, keep a few gallons of water in your pantry or basement.

If you want to keep drinking water fresh for an extended time, store it only in food-grade plastic tubs with airtight lids. For best results, clean your containers with dish soap on a regular basis and thoroughly rinse them before refilling them with water. If you do not have enough clean containers to hold your entire water supply, you can store water in many-gallon jugs before moving it to buckets. Buy professionally bottled drinking water rather than tap water whenever possible to ensure that the quality is reliable and safe to consume. Alternatively, if you are concerned about the safety of your tap water, you may want to consider purchasing a reverse osmosis filter.

Always keep a manual can opener and other tools with your food storage units so that you and other members of your household can enjoy the contents of your pantry when you're not cooking.

If the situation calls for it, keep multiple water purification tablets on hand as an extra precaution when mixing clean drinking water with polluted or suspicious water sources. Alternatively, these pills may be used to clean the plastic container that holds your drinking water before refilling it with fresh water.

Even if you grow your own vegetables and fruits, know how to shoot in a survival situation, and keep a large water supply in your pantry or basement, you should exercise caution. To avoid going outside during a crisis, you must still have enough food stored.

If you follow the guidelines outlined thus far, you should have no trouble achieving total self-sufficiency for yourself and your family. Refrigerate or freeze foods high in carbohydrates, protein, vitamins, fiber, fat, minerals, antioxidants, and beneficial cholesterol. Dry fruits and canned goods with longer shelf lives, such as dried fruit and canned goods, should be stored near the bottom of your storage shelves so you can use the freshest edibles before they expire.

Finally, keep fresh water in food cans with airtight lids to prevent contamination. If you do your research, store your water properly, and replenish your food supplies every few months, you should be able to survive any type of disaster without relying on outside assistance.

# WATER

Water is one of the most important things that a person should have on hand in the event of an emergency or natural disaster. People who do not drink enough water may perish in a matter of days.

If possible, gather as much information as possible before a disaster strikes, just as you would for any other emergency. Investigate your neighborhood and the areas most likely to be affected by natural disasters such as floods, hurricanes, earthquakes, and other natural disasters. These factors may have a significant impact on where you keep your water reserves.

The amount of water you will need to store is entirely dependent on your personal requirements. Different factors will influence how much water you should keep on hand. Each person's weight and level of activity influence how much they drink on a daily basis. People drink more in warm places than in cold ones, especially in the winter. Furthermore, the larger the number of people living in your home, the more water you will need to keep.

Recommendations in general for drinking and sanitary purposes, one gallon of water per person per day is recommended.

An adult requires at least half a gallon of water per day for drinking, cooking, and sanitation in order to maintain a regular activity level. Pregnant or breastfeeding women, the sick, and the elderly would all require more water.

It is not the time to figure out what works best for your family during an emergency or crisis. Save the amount of water recommended for each person ahead of time. If you are forced to ration water in an emergency, you will have a sufficient supply of water to draw from.

## Water Purification Techniques

The quality of water will vary dramatically depending on the quality of the source. If the water runs through a crack in the sidewalk or near an old gas station, it may contain lead or other pollutants. Once these chemicals are in our drinking water, they pose serious health risks, including genetic mutations and cancer.

Water may be cleaned in a variety of ways. Your water will determine the approach or procedures you use. Source, the volume of freshwater you have to cleanse, and any potential pollutants. Majority of the time. These two processes, filtration and purification, should be combined. Filtration eliminates the "chunks" from materials, while purification eliminates tiny elements like germs and viruses. Silt and other natural particles in your water. You should use more caution in times of emergency. You already have a catastrophe on your hands. It could be difficult to get medical help. Don't risk making a bad situation much worse by using your water.

## Filtration and Disinfection

The water you collect from natural sources will need to be filtered and disinfected. The terms filtration and disinfection are sometimes used interchangeably, but they mean different things. When you disinfect your water, you are killing any pathogens or viruses that may be present. When you filter it, you're removing parasites and larger debris from the water. Let's take a look at how we can accomplish both in an emergency.

How should you filter a bucket of dirty water from a wild source and make it drinkable? The short answer is that you must construct a filtration system. Begin with plastic bottles, preferably two-liter plastic bottles. To begin, cut the bottoms of the bottles and place a coffee filter on top, making sure the lid is screwed on tightly. Next, you'll need to construct the filter, which you can do with common household items or items found in DIY stores. First, apply a thin layer of activated charcoal, followed by an inch or two of fine grain, and finally, gravel (the smaller the gravel, the better). This should be sufficient to filter your water, but you can test it by adding coloring to the water and running it through your DIY water filter; if the water comes out clean, it has been properly filtered. This is a simple water filter because it only requires common household items; however, you will need to change the filter regularly or whenever the water runs slower than usual or does not filter properly.

We will be able to kill any bacteria or pathogens that have passed through the filter by disinfecting it. Boiling the water should be enough to make it safe to drink. Another excellent disinfection method is the use of ultraviolet rays.

Simply place the clear, bottled water in the sun to filter your water using solar disinfection. Make certain that any labeling on the bottle has been removed and that the bottle is clear and not colored. You must still ensure that the water has been properly filtered before exposing it to the sun's rays. If you have access to a rooftop, this may be an even better location for your water bottles. You should expose them to the sun for the entire day. If the sun is not shining brightly or the sky is cloudy, the bottles should be left for two days. On the other hand, UV disinfection products are portable devices that are usually battery-powered or crank-powered. If you use one of these devices, all you need is a brief burst of UV light to disinfect the water. In an emergency, choose the crank-powered ones so that you don't have to rely on batteries. If all of these methods fail, you can use calcium hypochlorite, also known as pool shock. Look for 100% calcium hypochlorite and avoid anything containing other disinfectants. To disinfect the water with this, first, dissolve a teaspoon in two gallons of water and stir it with a wooden spoon. If you use a metal spoon, the solution will corrode it. Add the solution to the water once it has been thoroughly mixed. Keep in mind that the ratio here is one pint of the solution to twelve and a half gallons of water to be disinfected.

In an emergency, water is probably the most important resource. Being cautious and storing it ahead of time can greatly improve our chances of survival in an emergency situation.

The process of removing contaminants from water is known as filtration. Purifiers do the same thing, but they may also remove viruses. Mechanical filtration, activated charcoal filters, simple water filters, oxidizing filters, neutralizing filters, and microfilters are all included in this category.

## Distillation

When the water reaches the boiling point, distillers gather the water vapor as it condenses. Most disease-causing bacteria are killed by the procedure, and the majority of chemical pollutants are also gone. Unless the technology is particularly constructed to remove them, certain pollutants, including those that quickly convert into gases (like radon or components of gasoline), may stay in the water.

Due to the frequent removal of the water's inherent minerals and dissolved oxygen, some individuals may find that distilled water tastes bland. Distillation has several substantial downsides. Pesticides and insecticides have melting points below 212°F (100°C), which prevents them from being effectively removed by distilling and causes them to become more concentrated in your freshwater. Furthermore, distillation is expensive since it uses a great deal of electricity and fresh water. The distillation procedure is very cumbersome. The average household unit produces around a gallon of water every four to five hours.

## Osmosis in reverse

The majority of mineral salts and suspended material are removed from water using the reverse osmosis (RO) membrane process, which employs a very thin layer with minuscule holes. The semi-permeable barrier retains any absorbed and suspended substances while allowing clean water to pass through. To put it another way, reverse osmosis works by forcing water through a specific membrane that allows water molecules to pass through while blocking larger particles such as lead, chrome, and poison. In reality, reverse osmosis is very effective at purifying water of a variety of pollutants. In addition to total dissolved solids, this contains asbestos, radium, nitrates, pesticides, copper, chlorinated particles, VOCs, and fluoride. RO has the potential to eradicate Giardia lamblia, cryptosporidium, germs, and viruses. The use of osmosis and active carbon filtration to remove most pollutants and contaminants from your water supply is widely regarded as the best overall water treatment technique.

If you're thinking about becoming a prepper, you've probably heard about purifying water before drinking it. Saltwater is not drinkable, and most freshwater contains bacteria and parasites. Drinking contaminated water can result in serious gastrointestinal issues, dehydration, and even death. Waterborne illnesses can also cause dehydration, and some are even fatal. As a result, preparing for a disaster and purifying your water before consumption are critical.

Water is the most important item on your survival prep checklist. You can only live for about three days without water, which can severely limit your ability to make decisions. However, there are numerous methods for purifying water before consumption. Experts recommend that each person drink at least one gallon of water per day. Here are some possibilities:

# PREPPER'S LONG-TERM SURVIVAL GUIDE

Purifying water before consuming it when prepping for survival begins with locating your nearest water source. In a disaster, you can stay hydrated by drinking rainwater, snow, or ice. You can collect water from a stream, lake, or tree if there is no water supply. If there is no running water, you can filter water with coffee filters or towels before drinking. These homemade methods are excellent for removing debris from the water.

Although public water is generally considered safe to drink, there are several factors to consider. Water can be murky or have an unpleasant taste. Consider purchasing food-grade containers to store water if you intend to keep it for an extended time. If it is contaminated, discard it and replace it with clean water. Whether you're storing it for drinking or using it in cooking, it's critical to purify it first.

Boiling water can save your life in a survival situation. Boiling water necessitates the use of fuel-efficient cooking methods, such as solar cookers. However, boiling does not affect chemical contaminants. You must allow it to cool before drinking. You can also try bleach treatment for disinfection. While boiling water is an excellent option, it is insufficient. For the best results, combine several methods.

## Boiling

If you are burning wood for heat, then boiling water will be easier. Just boil the water for at least 10 minutes to kill any harmful organisms, but make sure it does not boil off too much. You can also use a solar oven or reflector to bring water to a boil if you have trouble getting enough fuel together to keep your fire burning.

Boiling the water is one of the safest methods you can consider for purifying your water. It is the best method to kill all harmful organisms that can affect your health. You can use different things to boil your water and make sure it reaches the boiling point. Leave the water to cool, and it is ready to use. If you want to improve its taste, you can add some salt.

## Chemical Treatment

Chemical treatment is simple and can be accomplished using common household items. Water can be treated with chlorine and iodine crystals without removing any sediment or particles that may be present. Simply set it aside for about 30 minutes before using it. The main disadvantage of this method is that there is no guarantee that your water will be safe to drink if the chemical treatment fails.

To disinfect the water you want to drink, you can use tablets containing iodine, chlorine dioxide, or other disinfectants. These tablets are available in pharmacies and online. Because each type of tablet works differently, read the instructions carefully. For example, add one part or pint of chlorine solution to 100 parts of water or 12.5 gallons. If the chlorine taste is too strong, leave the water to settle for a while.

Liquid chlorine is available in grocery stores and is simple to use if the instructions are followed precisely. Shake or stir the container thoroughly after adding the bleach to the water. Allow the water to sit for approximately 30 minutes before drinking.

## Iodine Tablets

Iodine tablets are designed to eliminate harmful bacteria in water. Instead of iodine, it is recommended that you use iodine tablets which are available in many grocery stores. Before using these

# WATER

tablets, you must read the instructions first since they are not good for pregnant women and people suffering from thyroid issues.

You can add about five drops of iodine to a liter of water you want to disinfect. Add 10 drops if the water is cloudy. Then stir the water and leave it to sit for about 30 minutes before using it. Do not over-apply the iodine to water.

### Bleaching

Household bleach is another effective solution you can use to purify your water. You should only use unscented chlorine bleach that is specially designed for sanitation and disinfection purposes. Scented bleaches with colors are not good for purifying your water. Leave the water to settle if it is cloudy before you apply the bleach. Use a filter to remove the particles from the water so that you can apply your bleaching solution. Per each gallon of water, make sure you add about six drops of bleach. If the water is cloudy, you can add more drops of bleaching solution. Stir the water together with the solution and leave it to sit for about 30 minutes. It is normal for the water to have some chlorine odor. Pour the water between two containers and leave it to sit for additional minutes if the chlorine taste is too powerful.

### The Risks of Drinking Unpurified Water

There are numerous reasons why you should avoid drinking unpurified water during your survival preparations. The most important aspect is the health risk associated with its consumption. Cryptosporidium and other biological contaminants are too small for our bodies to detect. These contaminants can cause everything from mild discomfort to serious illnesses and even death. While chlorine and iodine are effective at killing bacteria and viruses, some can cause comas or fatal illnesses. Fortunately, most of these bacteria and viruses can be killed with proper treatment.

While drinking water from a nearby stream may seem appealing, the risks of ingesting contaminated water are significant. If you're not sure what you can drink, read the label on the bottle and filter the water before drinking. Unpurified water is frequently contaminated with pathogenic bacteria and viruses. In an emergency, consuming unpurified water can result in life-threatening illnesses.

When disaster strikes, having access to clean, purified water is critical. Humans cannot exist without water. That is why knowing how to purify water for drinking in a disaster situation is critical. Water is used in almost every aspect of life, including cooking and drinking. You'll be far ahead of the average person if you can purify your water.

Drinking water from a tap is safe if it is clean and free of contaminants, but using it to treat a wound risks further damage. To protect yourself from this, use a clean water source in your prepping efforts. Just don't put too many jugs or cases of water in a single container.

During a survival situation, boiling water is a good way to protect yourself from these health risks. Although boiling water kills pathogens, bacteria, and viruses, it does not remove chemical pollutants. Boiling water kills bacteria, viruses, and parasites but does not remove chemical contaminants. You should also let it cool before drinking it. Finally, use bleach to sterilize the water.

# CHAPTER 2: HOW TO STORE IT?

# PREPPER'S LONG-TERM SURVIVAL GUIDE

**Water Storage and Handling**

When you are in a disaster, you must find containers to store your water for long-term use. After purifying your water, keep it in a clean plastic or sanitary glass containers. Plastic containers are recommended in a disaster since they are unbreakable and lightweight. Metal containers can corrode, affecting the water's taste and infecting it with bacteria.

Water is critical in human life. According to studies, a person can live up to about 60 days surviving on clean water only. You drink about two quarts of water per day. Therefore, you must make your calculations to determine the total amount of water you will need throughout the disaster until normal supplies are restored.

If a disaster hits you, one of the most important survival priorities is to find water and purify it, so it is safe to drink. Whether you experience a natural disaster in your home or somewhere else, you should know that the human body cannot survive beyond three days without drinking water. Therefore, make sure you have enough water to sustain you during the disaster.

If your water supply is still under your control, you need to ensure that it isn't mishandled. This includes protecting the containers from damage and protecting the contents by using a quality water filter or purification tablets.

Also, make sure that you keep all of your water storage containers tightly sealed to reduce the risk of contamination, and try to keep them in a cool dark place, so sunlight doesn't damage or spoil your water. A basement or root cellar protected from outside contaminants would be your best option for storage until you are ready to use it.

When it comes to storing water, only use what you need. If you have a well, this is simply because you know exactly how much is there, but for everyone else, guesswork is required unless they are willing to put an exact number on it. For short-term emergencies, one gallon per person per day is the best rule to follow, and one gallon per person per day for longer-term emergencies. Because

# WATER

water weighs 8 pounds per gallon, you can roughly estimate how much your family requires each day by multiplying the number of people in your home by 10 to 15 pounds. That means a family of two would require 20-30 pounds per day, while a family of four would require 40-60 pounds.

This number will change depending on the type of emergency and the number of days you expect to be without help, so keep it up to date. You could also try dividing your stored water into one-liter portions for single use, as most siphon pump filters require about 2 liters of water to operate. Another reason to use only what is needed is that any excess would be wasteful.

## Why Keep Water for Such a Long Time?

Extreme weather systems occasionally strike cities or towns, such as hurricanes, floods, and other natural disasters. Because of their actions, people may be left without power or running water for days or weeks. It is difficult to find clean water during a water-related emergency or outbreak.

Humans can go for weeks without food but only a few days without water.

The ideal strategy for an impending emergency is to collect and store a personal safe water supply that includes water for drinking, food preparation, and personal hygiene.

If your usual water source becomes unavailable or if you are unsure whether it is safe to drink, you will require an alternative clean water supply for drinking, cooking, and personal hygiene. Keep enough clean water on hand for each family member to use 1 to 1.5 gallons per day. Save enough money for at least three days of drinking and sanitation for each person. If you have two adults and one child, you should store a 12-week supply if possible.

## How to Store Water in a Survival Situation

Although you can last a few days without food in an emergency, your body needs water to function properly. Without clean drinking water, you could become dehydrated and suffer from several medical issues that might keep you from being able to defend yourself against looters. Ensuring you have enough safe drinking water available for everyone in your household during a crisis is important, so have several gallons stored in your pantry or basement.

Store drinking water only in food-grade plastic containers with airtight lids to keep it fresh for longer. For the best results, clean your containers with dish detergent and thoroughly rinse them before refilling them. If you don't have enough clean containers, you can store water in several gallon jugs before transferring it to buckets.

If possible, buy commercially bottled drinking water instead of tap water to ensure consistent quality and safety. If you are concerned about the safety of your tap water, you should consider purchasing a reverse osmosis filter.

To make it easier for you and others in your household to enjoy the contents of your pantry, keep a manual can opener and other utensils with your food storage containers. Consider keeping several water purification tablets on hand as an extra precaution, so you can always mix safe drinking water with contaminated or suspect water sources if necessary. You can also use these tablets to clean the plastic container in which your drinking water is stored before refilling it.

Even if you grow vegetables and fruit, know how to hunt in a survival situation, and have a generous water supply in your pantry or basement. You still need to have enough food stored so that you don't have to go outside during a crisis.

# PREPPER'S LONG-TERM SURVIVAL GUIDE

If you follow the guidelines that have been explored here, you should have no trouble keeping yourself and your family completely self-sufficient. Just remember to store food items high in protein, carbohydrates, fiber, fat, vitamins, minerals, antioxidants, and good cholesterol. Store foods with a long expiration date, like dried fruit or canned goods, on the bottom of your storage shelves, so you utilize the freshest ingredients before they expire.

As with all types of emergencies, you should gather as much information as possible before a disaster happens.

## How Much Water Should You Store?

For water storage volumes, there are a few common guidelines. According to conventional prepping thinking, you should stockpile 1 gallon of drinking water per person each day. This will also have adequate water for cooking. You may need more water if it's really hot outside, you're exercising hard, you're sick, or you have a disease like pregnancy or diabetes.

A liter of water per person per day is sufficient for sanitation. Washing and hygiene water do not require the same high standards as drinking water.

It is determined by the size of the pet. If they weigh more than 50 pounds, they will typically require more than a person. If they weigh less than 50 pounds, it could be as little as a half-gallon. When limiting the water supply, keep the drinkable water for the four-legged relatives. A pet's digestive tract can withstand water that would make a person extremely ill.

The amount of water you need to store is entirely dependent on you. Numerous factors will influence how much water you should keep on hand. Each person has a different weight and activity level, which influences how much they drink per day. People who live in warmer climates consume more alcohol than those who live in colder climates. Furthermore, the more people in your household, the more water you will need to store.

## General Water Storage Recommendations

A minimum of one gallon of water per person per day is required for drinking and sanitation. A normally active person requires at least half a gallon of water daily for drinking, cooking, and sanitation. More water will be required for children, nursing mothers, the sick, and the elderly.

An emergency or crisis is not when you should find out what works for your family. Be prepared in advance by storing the recommended amount of water per person. If you are forced to ration water during an emergency, you will at least have a reserve of water available.

## Water Storage Containers

When you store your water in containers, you should treat them with disinfectant to kill any harmful bacteria and other microorganisms that could reside inside. Chlorine is the most common chemical used for this purpose, and adding eight drops of bleach per gallon or two drops per liter of water will make it safe to drink.

Water can be stored in a variety of containers and in a variety of ways. You can either buy large plastic containers to keep outside and fill with tap water as needed, or you can buy commercially bottled drinks like juice and soda pop. These bottles can be cleaned and reused. If you intend to store water in plastic bottles, avoid containers with the numbers one or two on the bottom because they contain phthalates, which can leach into the water. Also, avoid using colored plastic bottles, which contain lead and can contaminate your water supply.

# WATER

Another option for water storage is to buy commercially bottled water that has already been sealed in sturdy plastic containers. These bottles are available almost anywhere, and they have already been disinfected, so you know the water is safe. It also makes it simple to grab and go if needed. Jugs made of a variety of materials, such as glass, plastic, and ceramic, can also be used as water storage containers. These can also be reused several times before becoming worn out. Because ceramic jugs are opaque, light cannot pass through them and cause algae growth or the development of bacteria that could make you sick.

Soft drink bottles (2 liters), juice bottles, and containers designed specifically for carrying drinking water are examples of containers that were once used to store beverages. If you're buying a water container, make sure it's food-grade/food-safe. Contact the manufacturer if you are unsure whether a storage container is food-grade. If you are unable to use a food-grade water storage container, ensure that the container you use meets the following requirements:

- It has a tightly closing top and is made of tough, indestructible materials (i.e., not glass).
- If possible, use a container with a thin neck or aperture to allow water to drain out.
- Do not bring containers that have previously been used to hold toxic liquids or solid chemicals (bleach, pesticides, etc.)
- Before using a water storage container, clean and sanitize it.

To reduce microbial exposure, open a container before use and refrigerate it if power is available. Keep the container up high and out of reach of children and dogs if you don't have access to refrigeration. Use water from unsealed containers within 1 to 2 days if possible.

You must plan ahead of time if you want to store water for an emergency. Water can be difficult to transport because it is both heavy and takes up a lot of space. Everyone can transport a gallon of water; the problem arises when additional items must be transported. There are some excellent products available that can assist you in transporting large amounts of water and would be an excellent addition to your survival kit. However, this does not change the fact that it is still heavy and occupies a lot of space.

Having access to even a small reserve of water is extremely important, but moving large quantities of it, especially in an emergency, is not very feasible. But if you keep a static water storage, you will find it easier to collect some if you need to evacuate in a hurry. However, if you have a static source of water, you need to store it properly, so it doesn't go rancid and make sure you rotate your water at least every six months.

**Making Water Plan**

When you have a backup plan, you still have plenty to fall back on if your primary survival method fails. Additionally, having two backups is much better! If you have enough water in storage, you will have the time to reach it and purify it without having to take risky shortcuts. Two-to multiple supplies should be kept on standby for your household. Given the significance of water to your existence, a four-layered strategy is prudent:

- Possess a method for obtaining and purifying it at home.
- Store water for drinking.
- Use less water.
- If you really are away from home, have a technique to get and purify it.

Contrary to popular belief, filling up any leftover jugs you may have laying around is not the first step in creating a water strategy. Instead, it's to take a seat and carefully consider your predicament. Be truthful in your evaluation. By overestimating the amount of cash, you have on hand or the amount of memory space you can dedicate, you won't be doing yourself any favors.

**How to Make a Water Containment System**

In the best-case scenario, you'll have a water container to store your water with you in the wilderness. However, suppose you don't have a container. You'll have to think of another way to make a water container out of materials you can find. The first type of container you can make is a wooden crate. Look for a large enough dry wood or branch to hollow out and use as a water container. Carving a bowl-shaped hole on an even flat surface becomes easier if you have a cutting tool that can cut it in half lengthwise. Select a healthy-looking log with no rotten or cracked sections.

The next step is to start a fire and wait for the wood to become red hot. Cut a piece of wood in half to make a pair of thongs for carrying the coal safely. Place a few pieces of coal on the flat surface of the log. Then start blowing on the coals to keep them burning until a hole in the wood is burned. Continue until you have a large enough hole to hold water. Scrape away splinters with a knife or a rock from your surroundings to smooth out the surface. To make your water container, repeat the procedure as often as possible.

Another option is to use birch bark if you happen to come across one in the area. Remove and peel the bark with a survival knife or chisel if you have one. Cut it as precisely as possible to make shaping a rectangular piece into a water container easier. The bark will then need to be heated over a campfire to become flexible enough to fold and shape.

Fold the corn flakes into tiny triangle shapes, then fold them again to form a rectangular hollow bowl to hold water.

Secure the sides with a clip to keep the bark from unfolding. To make a clip, cut a tiny stick lengthwise, halfway, or less in the middle. Two pieces will suffice to hold the folded sections of bark in place and keep them from reopening.

If you come across a bamboo stalk, cut a sealing junction in it and use it to make a cup. Water containers can also be made from animal skins. To do this, wash the stomach of any large animal several times with water. Bring some water to a boil, then immerse the stomach in it for two hours, off the heat. Repeat the procedure as many times as necessary until the water in which the stomach has been soaking becomes clear.

After that, invert the stomach and scrape the insides, being careful not to puncture it. To make scraping easier, do this when your stomach is warm. After that, immerse your stomach in boiling water for 30 minutes. Finally, tie one end of the stomach together to form a pouch for water storage and seal the top.

Other plant materials, such as coconut shells, can be used to make water bottles, but a small cork carved from a short branch is required to seal the opening. You must remove all of the inside pieces to leave the shell hollow. The fruit will rot otherwise. The outside wooden section should be smoothed off to remove any splinters.

# WATER

## Testing Well Water

When it comes to testing your well water after a flood or other natural disaster, you want to keep the following in mind:

You should test the water at least seven to ten days after disinfection to ensure that the plumbing system has completely flushed the chlorine.

Until you have the well water tested, you should continue to boil it for one minute before using it or look for an alternative source of clean water.

You can contact your local health department or state laboratory certification officer for water sampling and testing information. Both options can put you in contact with a certified lab near you.

If the test results return positive for any coliform bacteria, you should repeat the good disinfection process and have the water tested again.

If the tests continue to show a presence of bacteria, then you should talk to your local health department for assistance in making your well water safe again.

You should then follow up with two more water tests. The first in two to four weeks and the second in three to four months.

Check the safety of your water in the long term by continuing to monitor bacterial quality at least twice a year or more often if you suspect a change in the water quality.

Now that we know what you need to do to be prepared for a disaster regarding food and water, as well as what to do after a disaster occurs, you're likely a little overwhelmed. There is no need to feel like this is an impossible task. Next, we'll look at how you can get started with preparing food and water storage for a potential disaster.

## Water Sources in and around Your Home

In a crisis, you should use any source of water you find around your home. The following are some of the sources you can consider in your home.

### Water heaters

You can use your water heater as a source of water during an emergency, depending on its size. Other water heaters are close to 200 gallons and can provide enough water for a few days if stored properly. Turn off the power and wait for the tank to cool. Place a bucket beneath the tank to collect water and use a drain valve. You should not turn on the tank until the main water supply has been restored.

Similarly, you can drink water from the toilet tank rather than the bowl. However, if chemicals have been added to the tank, you must first purify the water. When the water supply is interrupted, it does not come to an abrupt halt. As long as there are no leaks, water pipes can hold some water. Turn on the faucet at the highest point in your home to release pressure from the plumbing system. Then, to drain the water, turn on the lowest faucet.

### Melted Ice cubes

When you run out of drinking water, ice cubes made from clean water in your freezer can serve as a substitute. All that is required is to melt them, and the water is safe to drink. Depending on its quality, you may not need to purify it. Consider using the liquid from canned vegetables and fruit when all else fails.

### Swimming Pools' Water

If you have other drinking sources, you can use water from swimming pools for other purposes, such as personal hygiene. However, if you have no other choice, you can purify this water and drink it. There is no such thing as unsafe drinking water. All you have to do is use an efficient purification method to make the water safe to drink.

Following the safety precautions recommended by your city or region's authorities is critical. When a disaster disrupts the water supply system, you may need to turn off the main valve to prevent contaminants from entering the pipes.

### Water from the tap

If you are on a treated municipal or national water system, water plants may occasionally fail, allowing pollutants into the water system, or a natural disaster such as a flood, hurricane, or earthquake can cause your source of water to become polluted and unsafe to drink. In these cases, your primary goal should be to make the tap water drinkable. Boiling the drinking water is frequently used as a temporary fix until your public water authority can restore the purity of your drinkable water.

If your water is cloudy, run it through a basic coffee filter to remove some of the impurities before boiling it.

Normally, boil the water for 10 minutes before allowing it to cool completely. In general, this is the safest way to eradicate any disease or organism. A heat source, such as a fire or a tent emergency stove, as well as a camp pan or cup, is required to boil water.

Bring the water to a rolling boil for at least 60 seconds, plus one minute for every 1000 feet of elevation, to ensure that all living organisms are killed. If the water after boiling tastes flat, rehydrate it by transferring it between clean containers.

If the water is still murky or tastes off (don't drink it), you'll need to employ additional water treatment techniques before using it. Water purification pills are the most portable and lightweight alternative. Chlorine Dioxide and Iodine pills are the two most frequent forms.

## CHAPTER 3: YOU'LL NEVER RUN OUT OF WATER: RENEWABLE WATER SOURCES

Water service restoration could take several days or weeks. If your service is down, you may need to rely on safe water sources in nearby towns. If this isn't an option, you might be able to get water from a neighbor's well. Water stored in a well will also provide a safe source of water in the event of a disaster. Before drinking, always boil it. Other water sources include rainwater and the liquid from canned fruits and vegetables.

If you have a private well, you may not have enough drinking water. Consider bottled water or other safe water sources during an emergency. Remember that water from your radiator or boiler is not safe to drink; instead, use bottled water or water from another safe source. If you have an aquifer or a well, you should avoid drinking the water as well because floodwater can contain chemicals. Contact your local health department if you have any concerns about the safety of the water in your well. They will provide you with specific advice.

# WATER

Regardless of availability, bottled water is the best option during a disaster. Drinking bottled water is safer, especially if you are concerned about your health. Drinking contaminated water for personal hygiene, cooking, washing dishes, or bathing should be avoided regardless of taste or smell. Inquire with your local emergency officials about proper water sanitation. As a final precaution, closing the main water valve prevents contaminants from entering your home's plumbing system. If you're not sure about your local water supply, keep at least three days' worth of water in your home. Keep four liters of water per person on hand, and check the container's seal and storage area every six months. You should also be aware of the location of your water supplier and keep up with local news. There is always the possibility of a disaster, so it is best to be ready for anything.

## Finding a Safe Water Source in the Wilderness

You must understand the natural environment to find a safe water source in the wilderness. You should be familiar with the terrain and the habits of the animals. Look for dense vegetation, insect swarms, animal tracks, and new plants such as cattails, willow trees, and sycamore trees. In addition, keep an eye on the sky from time to time, as birds are known to flock to water sources in the early morning.

Streams, lakes, and rivers are the best water sources in the wilderness. However, before drinking them, make sure they have been cleaned with water purification products or filters. Boil the water before drinking it for the best results. Remove all debris from the water to avoid contamination. If you can't find a stream, collect rainwater or plant water instead. Urine is also a good water source, and it can last several days.

When looking for a water source, look upstream first. Higher water tables indicate cleaner water. On the other hand, fresh mountain streams may contain contaminants carried upstream. Clean the water first for the best results. Then proceed to walk downhill. Water is abundant in the valley bottoms. However, you should never drink water found upstream because it is likely to be contaminated. So, if you come across a stream or a waterfall, be prepared to spend some time digging.

Puddles are an excellent natural source of water. They are most commonly found on large rocks or in the crooks of trees. If you see water trapped in crevices, look for springs. Bacteria may be present in puddles. If you collect water from a puddle, filter it before drinking it. If water is stagnant, bacteria and other microorganisms that may be present can multiply rapidly.

Water is essential for survival, so finding a safe water source in the wilderness is critical. The human body cannot function properly without water. Dehydration can have an impact on both mental and physical health. Recovery can even take up to three days. On the other hand, water in the wilderness is dangerous and should be purified before drinking. If you can't drink it, try boiling it for one minute.

## Rainwater

If you have a small garden, collecting rainwater can be a great way to store enough drinking water to last for months. Rain barrels are an excellent option for collecting water and are cheap and environmentally friendly. If you don't have a water system, capturing rainwater can save you a lot of money in water bills. Rain barrels can be set up to capture rainwater and feed pressure washers or garden hoses. Not only can you use rainwater for washing clothes, but you can even bathe yourself and your pets.

If you're collecting rainwater for survival prepping, you'll need a rain barrel, a rain funnel, and a filter. While this method is useful when camping, it's not the best solution for collecting rainwater. If it becomes contaminated, it will be unsafe for consumption and serve as a breeding ground for mosquitoes. It also takes up valuable space in your container, so you should consider collecting rainwater in several different locations.

Collecting rainwater for survival prepping is easy and inexpensive. There are simple systems for collecting rainwater, and more advanced ones can be complicated. However, the key is to collect as much water as possible. A rain barrel will provide you with clean water for washing, bathing, and sewage purposes. Collecting rainwater is an excellent option because not everyone lives in an area with abundant rainfall. Certain natural disasters may cause people to be forced to leave their homes.

You can also use a tarp as a funnel for collecting rainwater. Place a bucket at the base of the tarp to collect rainwater. You might find neighboring homes with materials to harvest rainwater if you're lucky. They may even be willing to share. If you don't, try to use the tarp and pipes that you've collected from them. These can also be made of scavenged material.

The majority of places in the world have dry and rainy seasons, so it is important to know how to store water to sustain yourself in these conditions. A properly built cistern can store up to three daily gallons per person. The World Health Organization has published a PDF on water supplies and survival, which says that a person needs only 2.5 liters of water per day. If this number is not met, an emergency supply of water will last for at least several days.

For those who are concerned about hygiene, rainwater harvesting can be an excellent backup source of water. Even one inch of rain on a square foot can yield about 0.623 gallons of clean water, which is enough to drink. It will quickly fill a small storage tank. Several dozen or hundreds of square feet of roof space in a larger area will yield plenty of rainwater.

Besides being a free water source, rainwater collection systems can help you prepare for any disaster or emergency. A household rainwater collection system will store hundreds of gallons of water after a few days of moderate rainfall. It is important to purchase a rainwater harvesting system that can be easily operated and used. While rain rarely falls hard enough to yield a significant quantity of water, the rain that does fall is usually not consistent enough to provide a meaningful amount of water.

The importance of rainwater as a backup water supply for survival preppers goes beyond drinking water. You can use rainwater for washing vehicles, dishes, and even people and pets. The water can even be used to flush the toilet. The possibilities are endless, and rainwater can serve as your primary water source and a backup for your existing supplies. The use of rainwater is so widespread that it can be used for nearly any task that requires water.

**Rivers, Streams, or Lakes**

Water may be abundant in rivers or lakes in your area, depending on your location. Most local governments get their tap water from reservoirs such as lakes, dams, or even streams. The only distinction is that the water has been purified. Water from these sources is frequently contaminated with chemicals, livestock waste, human sewage, and other potentially harmful contaminants. Before using the water for drinking or other hygiene purposes, it must be purified and treated with appropriate chemicals to kill harmful germs.

# WATER

For survival reasons, avoiding standing water in rivers, streams, and lakes is critical. Wetlands serve as breeding grounds for insects that require stagnant water to reproduce. These creatures also provide food and nutrients to other freshwater animals. Wetlands are made up of various types of water. Swamps, bogs, marshes, flood plains, prairie potholes, and other features are examples. These habitats can be found all over the world and are frequently found near bodies of water.

## Creeks and Ponds

You can use surface water obtained from creeks and ponds if you cannot access underground water. If possible, try to move upstream to get surface water, especially from inhabited places. Try to avoid shallow ponds if there are bigger sources. When the water is dark, produces odor, and contains floating particles, this can indicate that it is polluted. Unless you thoroughly purify it, contaminated water is dangerous to your health. Therefore, always exercise extreme caution if you suspect that the water you're using is contaminated.

## Collecting Groundwater

Collecting groundwater for survival has several advantages. First and foremost, you will have access to clean water. You can also store large amounts for extended periods. Second, you can test the water for harmful toxins and use it to treat illnesses caused by drinking it. Whatever method you choose, you'll need to collect groundwater for survival prep. Several benefits of collecting groundwater are listed below. Continue reading to learn more about these advantages.

Water is one of the most basic needs in a disaster or emergency, and survivalists can access a wide range of freshwater sources. These sources could include springs, rivers, or lakes. If the water is salty or brackish, distilling it before drinking can help you avoid bacterial exposure. Water from precipitation can also be collected for drinking, but be careful not to allow it to fall through the jungle canopy! New snow can also be safely melted and consumed without further treatment.

While drinking water is essential, you must also consider how to obtain, treat, and transport water in an emergency. Water should be collected from a flowing source, according to experts. If that source is unavailable, you can gather contaminated water on your own. Collecting toxic water in a water storage area can also save your life during a disaster. If you intend to bug out, gather water from any available source that is safe for drinking and cooking.

## Finding Hidden Sources of Water

There are many places to find hidden water sources, and it's easy to overlook them. They can be inside your home or out. It all depends on your location and what you're most comfortable doing. Water sources can quickly become stagnant, so finding ways to purify them is a must. Make sure you store the water in containers that are approved for this purpose. Once you've found hidden water sources, you'll be well prepared if disaster strikes.

Fresh fruit is a great source of water. While it's not always possible to grow fruit in your area, many fruits are ripe and packed with water. Fresh fruit is best for survival purposes, as it has a high moisture content. Look for fruits that are rich in water content, like pears or coconuts. Keep in mind that if you're in a tropical climate, coconuts can be difficult to grow, but you can find them in your grocery store.

Another way to find water is to watch for animal tracks or bird droppings. During the early morning hours, you'll find animal tracks; in the evening, you may find bird droppings on the ground. In the desert, animal tracks are easy to spot, and they almost always lead to water. Birds will typically flock to water sources, so watch for these signs and collect water. If the SHTF hits, you won't have to wait long to gather water.

You can also find water in dry areas. Some dry areas are covered with water-loving plants and can be a great water source. You can even find hidden sources of water by digging in riverbeds. But this will probably be messy and require some sort of filtering, so you'll have to be prepared to clean the water. It's always better to be prepared than to be without water.

# BOOK 5: HYGIENE

## Chapter 11: Hygiene

Personal hygiene will be one of those things that will deteriorate the longer you are in survival mode. The scarcity of hygiene products, and lack of sewer line cleaning, will make your hygiene harder to maintain. The good news is that your body, particularly your nose, will get used to it rather quickly. Let us go through the different sections of hygiene and ways to mitigate certain issues.

## Supplies

Keeping yourself and your surroundings clean is essential not only for your sanity but also for your health. Personal hygiene supplies, cleaning supplies, and trash and waste disposal supplies will be required. Here's an illustration of a list.

### Shampoo/Conditioner

Not having hair supplies may not seem like a big deal at first, but not washing your hair has long-term consequences. Your hair may begin to smell, your scalp may become itchy, and bacteria may accumulate.

Conditioner's primary function is not to clean your hair, but to keep it strong and healthy. Shampoo and conditioner bars are available if storage space is an issue. You should also keep some dry shampoo on hand. The dry stuff isn't good for your hair in the long run, but it's okay for now and then.

### Clippers for Nails

Unless you clip your nails, they will continue to grow. Dirt and bacteria can accumulate under long fingernails and toes. They can also catch on things, and if you rip them out by accident, you'll have a medical problem.

### Paper Towels

Toilet paper is always one of the first things people buy in an emergency. Maintain a good stockpile for these occasions and times when you can't get to a store. However, be wary of using too much storage space for TP because it isn't a necessary item. It's more of a convenience. If you're in a pinch, you can always clean yourself with a clean cloth, sponge, or paper.

Deodorant isn't an "essential" item if you don't care about the smell, but it can definitely make you more comfortable in stressful situations.

### Menstrual Cups/Tampons

Tampons and pads, while technically a luxury item, are extremely useful to have on hand in an emergency. A menstrual cup is a great option if you want something more long-term. You won't have to worry about running out of pads or tampons because these can be washed and reused for 1-2 years.

### Wipes and antibacterial soap

Antibacterial soap is required to kill bacteria. Soap in the form of a bar is less expensive, but it requires slightly more water, so keep that in mind. Antibacterial wipes can be used instead of soap to protect your water supply as much as possible. Keep in mind that antibacterial soap does not kill viruses.

# HYGIENE

### Sanitizer for Hands

Hand sanitizer is a germ-killing alternative to hand washing. While washing your hands with soap and water is still considered the best option, it isn't always possible. According to the CDC, hand sanitizer must contain at least 60% alcohol in order to be effective. Some people make their own, which is fine as long as they adhere to the 60% rule.

### Bleach

Bleach is an effective cleaner that can kill 99.9% of bacteria. It's usually diluted and can harm your lungs, so make sure you understand how to use it properly.

### Borax

Borax is another strong cleaner that is frequently used to remove mold. Because it's a natural alternative to bleach, you probably don't need to stockpile both for cleaning. Borax is also very inexpensive and can be used for a variety of tasks such as laundry, weed control, pest control, sanitizing, and more.

### Vinegar, White

White vinegar, a cheap basic, has a variety of uses, including dishwashing and disinfecting your home. It's been used for centuries but has one drawback: it's not as effective at disinfecting as commercial cleaners. If that's really important to you, you might want to invest in a more powerful cleaner.

### Wipes Disinfectant

Disinfectant wipes from brands like Clorox or Lysol are ideal for quick cleanup and sanitization. Please keep in mind that these are not intended for your hands or body.

### Detergent for Laundry

Keeping your clothes clean and fresh is essential for your appearance and health. Your skin's oil soaks into your clothes, attracting all kinds of bacteria. If you continue wearing those clothes, you may experience itching and infection. Stockpile detergent and soap for washing clothes so that you don't run out of soap for yourself.

### Doodie Toilet Paper Bags

These bags are made specifically for human waste. They're tough, puncture- and leak-proof, and can last a day for a family of four. In an emergency, they are used for all types of portable toilets.

### Cat Litter

Did you know that kitty litter can also be used to treat human waste? You don't want to empty your makeshift toilet bags when they aren't full, but they don't like sitting around all day. Sprinkle some kitty litter on the bottom of your new bag and again after you've used it. The litter will absorb odors and help to mask them. To kill germs, you can also apply borax or bleach. In the event of a snow emergency, kitty litter can also be used for traction!

# PREPPER'S LONG-TERM SURVIVAL GUIDE

### Garbage Bags, Heavy Duty

In an emergency, trash bags are critical. You'll need heavy-duty ones to keep your trash contained. If trash isn't contained and spreads everywhere, it attracts all kinds of pests, bacteria, and, eventually, disease.

### Personal Cleanliness

Personal hygiene is always possible as long as you have enough water. Of course, using the stored water to clean yourself is never as easy or as comfortable as hopping in the shower, but it's doable. It will be ideal if you have a river or a pond near your house so that you can take your baths there, but remember to use biodegradable soaps to avoid adding any unnecessary chemicals to the natural water. If you don't have a clean water source next to your house, you can always use camp showers to stay clean and maintain your hygiene.

Solar showers are a good idea. Simply fill the tank with clean water, hang it on a stable tree branch, and leave it to warm up. You can then simply open the nozzle to enjoy a warm outdoor shower. Despite that, the real issue is cleaning your dishes and making sure you get rid of all germs and bacteria. This is when an electric dishwasher is handy in the city, as these devices help sanitize eating utensils, and we take them for granted. However, when you're living off-grid, it will be necessary to heat the water you use for cleaning the dishes. Make sure you use enough soap and that you gently rinse the dishes in a light bleach solution. This step is particularly important for sanitizing eating utensils, especially if you live with a larger group of people.

### Washing Your Hands, the Right Way

It is critical to keep your hands clean. When cleaning your hands, there are a few important steps to take to avoid illness.

Wet your hands with either running water or stored water.
Cover your hands with soap or gently rub a bar of soap between your hands, massaging all parts. Scrub your hands for at least 20 seconds before wetting them again or removing the soap. Check the backs of your hands, wrists, under your fingernails, and between your fingers.
The next step is to thoroughly rinse your hands to remove all of the soap.
If you're using running water, turn it off with your elbow.
Finally, make sure to dry your hands and avoid touching anything unsanitary.

### Oral Hygiene and Health

These are all the tips you need to save water while brushing your teeth or using any other different method. This is also for people wondering how they can brush their teeth or use toothpaste without running water. Here's how it's done.

Using a reusable cup is the most important part of brushing your teeth without running water. Some people even do it to conserve water and maintain non-renewable resources. Using a cup filled with clean water will help you rinse your mouth and get rid of the toothpaste. You just need to use all the water in the cup without wasting any. You'll also need a sink with working plumbing, a bowl to spit the water out, or any place where you can comfortably rinse out your mouth.

Make sure you use a clean and sanitized toothbrush and wash it after every use. Don't use your hands instead of a cup, as this will waste a lot of your water supply. You should also remember to floss regularly. Just because you live outside of society doesn't mean you can let your dental health decline.

## Feminine Hygiene

All you need for feminine products and menstruation is a reusable menstrual cup and clean water. Douching and feminine products, particularly scented ones, are harmful to your health. You should only clean these areas with water and use tampons or menstrual cups to control blood flow. To be prepared, keep a warm bucket of clean water nearby during your menstruation days. When it comes to your private areas, you can use wet wipes on the areas around your thighs, but all you need is clean water.

## Wounds and Injuries Cleaning

Living off the grid entails spending more time outside than inside. This also means you'll have more open wounds and injuries. Unfortunately, medical assistance may not be available if you live outside of the city. You must learn how to clean and sanitize your wounds before they become infected with bacteria. This is when sanitation can mean the difference between life and death.

To begin, clean water is always required to clean any open wounds. Some of your drinking water will suffice if you're outside and don't have access to a water source. You can also look for a nearby river or natural water source to clean your wound and wash away any blood. The next step is to sterilize your wound, which will require the use of a sterilizer or another solution. If you don't have any sterilizer, urine should suffice. You can also use surgical powder, but avoid putting any baby powder on your wounds.

After cleaning your wound, keep it covered and avoid exposing it to the elements. Any contact with dust or insects can cause infections, so cover it with a cloth until you can get home or access first aid supplies. If your wound is large and requires immediate attention, use plantain leaves as bandages because they have antibacterial and anti-inflammatory properties.

## Taking Care of Babies When Living Off-Grid

Babies require a significant amount of attention under all circumstances. It's not very different in the wilderness. If you have a baby, you'll need to keep them clean at all times to prevent infections. In fact, babies should be given even more care and attention when you live off-grid. This means that you should change and clean their diapers more regularly. This includes times when they only pee. Your baby will be more prone to infections and bacteria when you live in a natural environment, as they will be more exposed to germs, dust, and unsanitary things. This is why you always need to have wet wipes on hand to prepare for unexpected emergencies. Make sure you find a clean area to change your baby's diapers. If you're outside, lay down a clean cloth to protect your baby from dirty surfaces.

## Toilet Facilities

If you stay indoors, in a home, or any other place with a toilet, you will have no trouble flushing after you have used it in the short term. Flushes can still be used even when there is no power; simply manually fill the tank. However, this will cease to function once sewer lines are no longer cleaned and waste has nowhere to go. You should prepare for such an occurrence.

# PREPPER'S LONG-TERM SURVIVAL GUIDE

Although chemical toilets may be a viable option, they may not be sustainable in the long run due to the need to store large quantities of whatever chemical is used to treat the waste. That leaves us with much simpler solutions, the first of which is buckets. Buckets can be found and purchased at any hardware store. You can add your own toilet seat to a five-gallon bucket or larger, which will end up being a relative luxury. Add some sand to the bottom of the bucket and keep the sand source nearby with a scoop so you can cover the waste. If you have baking soda or laundry detergent, you can sprinkle some on top, but you're probably better off saving those for other things. Every member of your family or group should ideally have their own bucket, and once it is half full, you must dispose of the waste, or it will become too heavy to move around. If buckets and sand aren't an option, heavy-duty bags can do the job; however, these must be emptied more frequently because you don't want the bag to burst open while you're trying to move it.

You can also dig a hole or a latrine, but this is significantly more work. If you do decide to dig a latrine, make it wide enough (about two or three feet) and deep enough (also two or three feet). Cover the waste with a scoop of earth or dirt after you've used it.

Because toilet paper does not last forever, you will eventually need to consider a solution. Magazines and newspapers are excellent options, but old clothes, such as t-shirts or socks, will last longer because they can be washed. It is always important to wash your hands after using the restroom, but it is especially important in survival situations like this. It is critical that you wash your hands, whether with sanitizer or in a river. If you use sanitizer, keep in mind that you will have alcohol in your hands immediately after using it; avoid going near open flames or other flammable components, or you may catch fire.

If you don't have your own septic system or working plumbing, using the bathroom while living off the grid can be dangerous. This is because your or your family's waste must be properly disposed of for sanitary reasons. However, there is no need to be concerned. If you don't have access to working plumbing, you have a few other options.

Digging a pit toilet behind your house is one of the most sanitary options. If this sounds like a solution for you, make sure you have plenty of sawdust on hand to cover up the feces after you're finished. Another excellent option for keeping the pit clean and sanitary is lime. Make sure to use lime every time you use the pit. Some people may have toilets without running water in their off-grid homes. If you are one of these people, you can use the toilet as long as you have enough water to flush the waste every time you use it.

Another thing to think about is how you'll use toilet paper. Toilet paper rolls are always available. However, you will eventually run out of them, so you must find a replacement. For the most part, any type of paper will suffice. You can also use leaves, but be cautious of poison ivy. You and everyone in your household must also wash your hands. Even if you don't have running water, you can keep your hands clean by using alcohol-based hand sanitizers or sanitary wipes.

**Laundry**

This is one of those things that you might only remember to do after a week or so into an emergency situation, but in the long term can be quite important. Planning for it is just as essential as anything else, and with the right preparation, you can set yourself up well.

Hand washing your clothes can be both time and energy-consuming. However, you can make it easier by purchasing a large tub, a smaller tub, and a washboard. Fill up the large tub with water

# HYGIENE

and detergent, ideally a biodegradable one, and scrub. Place the washed clothes in a smaller tub with just water and hang them out to dry. It may be that you can't get hold of a washboard, if that is the case, you need to scrub them with your hands, slap them against a large rock, or anything hard and not particularly dirty, although this is less efficient.

You could achieve the same results with a large bucket, a lid, and a plunger. Make a hole in the lid, just large enough for the handle of the plunger to fit in, add water, and detergent and use the plunger to clean your clothes. You should use a little scrubbing brush just to take out the more stubborn stains.

**Waste Disposal**

We must be able to dispose of all of the waste that we produce. It's simple in today's society; we just put all of our trash in garbage cans and someone comes every week or so to pick it up. When you're in survival mode, it's a much bigger problem.

Let's start with the obvious. This is waste generated by people through food, packaging, or anything else that does not leave our bodies. Families, in particular, can generate a significant amount of waste. In an emergency, you should consider burning some of it, but you should also try to reuse it as much as possible. Plastic containers and tin cans can be used to make plant vases or as part of an alarm system. The more inventive you are, the less garbage you will generate. If you can't burn the rest, the next best option is to bury it somewhere far away from your current location. Also, avoid burying it near a body of water or your own crops, as the waste may become contaminated.

Human waste is a different type of waste that can be used for a variety of purposes. If you choose to dispose of it, bury it as far away from water sources as possible. Ideally, you would be digging and filling a latrine. Bury it once it's about two feet from the top and start a new one. You can also burn it, but you must let it dry for a few days first, which will intensify the smell. You could also mix it with flammable liquid to make it easier to burn. This, however, is not the best solution. Burying it is far preferable.

However, you should use some of the waste as garden fertilizer. This can help crops grow faster and healthier. However, if you do this, you must keep urine and feces separate. It is best to use a funnel to direct the urine into a jug or bucket for this.

To use urine in your garden, let it age for a few months before mixing it with dirty water from your laundry, for example. The mixture should be one part urine and eight parts water, and it should be poured directly into the garden.

When the bucket is full, add a lid with a hole and collect the feces separately. It would need to sit for about a year before it could be used for composting.

**Keeping Warm**

Clothing and shelter are two basic necessities, depending on the weather where you are, you could last a little longer without either, but in the long term, you wouldn't survive being exposed so much. Ideally, your home would still be standing and even without power or water, it would still be the best shelter. If your home was destroyed or unavailable to live in, the next best thing would be a family member's or friend's house. The important thing has a roof over your head and clothes to warm you up or protect you from the sun.

# PREPPER'S LONG-TERM SURVIVAL GUIDE

**Clothing**

Clothing should be prioritized because it is your first line of defense against the elements. Even if many of us have entire wardrobes and closets filled with various types of clothing, bringing them with you if you need to leave your home may not be the most practical thing to do.

In situations like this, you must choose a few outfits. You would need to prepare some clothes ahead of time because many of the clothes we wear today are impractical and provide little protection in an emergency. When packing clothes for an emergency, comfort, practicality, and durability should take precedence over fashion and style. Although this appears to be logical, most people have never been in an emergency situation and would most likely choose their favorite clothes over thinking logically.

Comfortable shoes are the best to wear in a survival situation. Thick socks will also protect you from cold, water, and other hazards in the wilderness. You should go for high quality here, as the cheap socks that most people buy will not last long with constant washing and use. Work boots that are thick and comfortable are also an excellent choice. Thick soles with ankle support are what you should look for. When the weather is nice, bring a pair of sneakers, especially if you plan on walking a lot. If you live in an area where it snows frequently, you should also invest in a pair of snow boots. Pants are also required. You'll need some sturdy jeans that are comfortable for walking and working in. These may be more difficult to hand wash and will take a long time to dry. Alternatively, cotton cargo pants are a great option; aside from being comfortable, they usually have a lot of pockets that will come in handy. A few pairs of shorts for when the weather gets warmer should also be in your emergency closet. However, you don't want them to be too short because they won't protect your legs as well. Add a couple of belts, even if you don't need them to keep your pants in place, because they can come in handy in other situations.

Choose tops that are durable and comfortable over fashionable ones. T-shirts, button-down shirts, flannel shirts, long-sleeve shirts, and sweatshirts should all be included.

Although underwear is not as important as the other items of clothing mentioned thus far, it is still something you should have on hand in an emergency. Underwear prevents sweat from getting to specific body parts such as the groins and is very easy to wash and dry. You should wear the same underwear for at least two weeks before washing them; otherwise, you will spend too much time washing clothes and too little time doing other important things.

Heavy coats, for example, have a place in your emergency closet. Especially if you live in an area where it frequently rains or snows. In fact, because the head is where we lose the most heat, covering it with a hood or a hat can keep us warmer for longer.

You'll need a pair of gloves that keep your hands warm while still allowing you to move your fingers freely. You should also include an inexpensive rain poncho, which can protect you from the rain. They are also easily foldable and light, so they won't take up much space. A good quality parka for harsh winters can really help you get through the colder months. If possible, choose one that allows you to remove the liner to make it warmer or cooler, depending on the weather. These are not cheap, but they are necessary if you live in extremely cold climates.

It is critical to dress in layers, especially when it is cold outside. Especially if you are performing household or physical tasks. You don't want to get too hot and sweat all over your clothes, especially if you take breaks and the sweat cools down. Layers allow you to easily remove and add cloth-

# ENERGY

ing while also managing your body temperature and avoiding overheating. Another thing to think about when preparing for an emergency is whether or not to bring camouflage clothing. Although this is great if you're out hunting, provided you have the appropriate camouflage for the environment, most people live in suburbia, which means your camouflage won't help you much. Just keep this in mind when shopping for clothes.

# BOOK 6: ENERGY

# ENERGY

# ARE YOU READY FOR A BLACKOUT ?

**The Blackout Survival Kit**

You should never ignore your blackout survival kit when you are bugging out of your house for the survival phase. So, the things you should count on adding to this kit are:

A perfect container or set of containers that are distinguished by colors. You can store the health items in a red-colored box, edibles in green, and everything else in specified colored boxes that you can remember. When the light goes out, you can find these boxes easily with your flashlight.

As you prepare the kit, take another big box with a yellow-colored lid over it. Keep the lighting objects in it, such as batteries, flashlights, power banks, radios, etc.

Keep several lighting options in that box and prefer to add an LED lantern in the kit on priority. Keep a few luminous sticks or bracelets in that box to help you with emergency lighting needs.

Keep a headlamp in the kit, which will help you wear it around your head at night time to work on some things around the shelter.

Add a voltage meter to the box to check the power capacity of the batteries.

Right next to the box, I prefer to keep a camping stove set, which will be useful for you when the stored solar power runs out to deprive you of using electrical cooking appliances.

Next time any challenge comes up and knocks at the door, you should not feel frightened anymore and just act prepared, which you actually are!

**Recommended Power Sources**

**Solar Panel System**

You must build or install your own solar panel system and transport the panels and other necessary items in a separate set of bags. If you are bugging out during the summers or springs, you will have plenty of sunlight to generate some power for charging the survival essentials.

If a difficult situation arises during the rainy or winter seasons, the amount of solar strength may be reduced, and you will have to rely on other power sources to meet the basic requirement. You can certainly transport solar panels and an inverter or equivalent equipment in your car, but the implementation is quite costly. If you have some extra cash, you can always get smaller solar panels to generate a limited amount of power for basic survival needs like charging flashlight batteries, emergency lights, and so on.

Solar panels have grown in popularity, particularly in recent years. Many people have solar panels installed in their homes and businesses. There are many cheap and affordable solar panels on the market that are also very efficient. It has significantly reduced their fuel and electricity consumption, allowing them to significantly reduce their bills. It is beneficial financially, but it has no negative environmental effects because it is a renewable energy source.

### Find a Reliable and Low-Cost Solar Panel

With the growth of the solar panel industry, there are many different types of solar panels on the market. It is difficult to find an affordable and effective solar panel. There are numerous types of solar panels available on the market. There are a few things to consider when purchasing solar panels. The first thing you should notice is the size. Consider your power consumption. If you have a large family, a larger panel is required, or you can purchase more than one.

Foldable solar panels, briefcase panels, and common makeup solar panels are examples of different types of solar panels. The first two are a little pricey. The latter, on the other hand, is both cost-effective and efficient. They are very popular monocrystalline cells. One of the most popular markets is for a Renogy 100W 16lb panel. It is not expensive and has a power rating of 100W. They are 47 24 inches in length. You can put them in your house, vacation cabin, or on top of your car.

In ideal conditions, you should place your solar panel in a single location. However, deciding on the ideal location is difficult. It would be beneficial if you could figure out where you can get the most power. A long connector cable will be required for this purpose. There are kits on the market that include all of the necessary accessories. They also include connector cables. That cable, however, is quite short. If you have a two-story building, a long cable will be required to connect the panel to the battery pack.

You can measure the distance and order the appropriate cable. Also, when selecting a cable, look for one with a weather-resistant covering that can withstand all types of weather. Most businesses manufacture cable that is compatible with their solar panels. Purchase those cables.

### **Geothermal Energy**

The MiniGeo is a modular geothermal power plant that is the size of a shipping container. Its output ranges from 100kW to 1MW, depending on the geology and demand.

In winter, geothermal energy is best used to warm up a building. In summer, the ground will absorb the warm air from your home and disperse it without creating any negative environmental impacts. Although geothermal energy is available worldwide, it's more readily available in some regions. Regions with natural hot water reservoirs are more likely to have geothermal power plants. Because geothermal energy is easily available and relatively cheap to access, geothermal power plants are most common in geologically active areas of the United States. Active volcanoes, tectonic plate boundaries, and areas with thin crust allow heat to escape.

These hot waters are brought to the surface through a production well. Once the hot water is released from the deep reservoir, it flashes into steam, turning turbines and generating electricity. However, geothermal power is still expensive to access. It is best suited for homes that have smaller energy demands.

The environmental benefits of geothermal systems are questionable. In contrast, earth energy methods are highly recommended for heating and cooling. They quickly pay for themselves, both in cash and environmental benefits. One example of a popular earth energy home heating solution is a heat pump. Heat pumps will pay for themselves within 5 to 7 years. Heat pumps move heat from one place to another and are a great choice for heating and cooling the home. Heat pumps can be used for the HVAC system, as well.

While geothermal energy is used to heat and cool buildings, the process can have detrimental effects on the environment. Using geothermal energy for electricity can cause surface hot springs and geysers to dry up, which can lead to land subsidence. The water from a geothermal cooling tower can contain natural substances, including boron and mercury. It also emits carbon dioxide, but the amounts are far less than those from a fossil fuel electrical generation facility of similar capacity.

## ENERGY

### Wind Energy

Wind energy is another efficient source of electricity. A turbine is made up of turbines that are moved by the wind, causing the internal generator to spin and produce electricity. This electricity is then routed into the system or stored in battery banks. Wind generation systems typically have lower installation costs than solar systems.

However, one disadvantage of using this energy source is that some areas do not receive much wind. Wind turbines may not be effective if you live in an area with many tall trees and other physical barriers. Another consideration is that if your turbine is located in an especially unsteady but windy area, you may not be able to generate a continuous and uninterrupted power supply. Wind turbines require large open spaces to function properly.

There are a few hurdles that homeowners must overcome before reaping the full benefits of wind power. These obstacles include obtaining permission to build a windmill and some areas' building height limits. However, if you have the right property, you might be able to install a small wind turbine and save a lot of money.

Wind turbines can generate electricity for homes in addition to being a natural energy source. The wind power generated by these turbines can be used immediately or stored for later use. Batteries and pumped-storage hydropower are two methods for storing the excess power generated by renewable energy.

Before deciding to install a home wind turbine, you should conduct extensive research on the amount of wind in your area. Check for zoning regulations, covenants, and potential neighbor protests. Next, calculate how much energy your home will require each year. Finally, determine the size of the tower and turbine required for optimal performance. Connect the home to the electrical grid once the wind energy is generated.

Wind turbines are an excellent renewable energy source that can be mass-produced in windy areas. They are typically installed on 100-foot-tall towers. These wind turbines occupy the space above them, which can be used for farming, construction, or the installation of additional wind turbines. Wind energy outperforms solar panels in terms of efficiency. In addition, unlike solar panels, wind turbines can generate electricity 24 hours a day, seven days a week. In fact, one wind turbine can generate the same amount of electricity as thousands of solar panels. The most significant advantage of wind turbines is that they do not require sunlight to function.

Wind turbines also generate electricity at night, when the wind is not as strong as solar panels and are less expensive. On the other hand, a solar panel requires a significant amount of electricity to function properly. But it's well worth the time and money.

### Micro-Hydro Electricity

If you do have one, then you must count on looking at the micro-hydro electricity source for powering your home. The hydroelectricity concept uses running water to generate electricity by utilizing the energy coming from the flow of water from high to low places.

The micro hydropower system has the working mechanism of converting the flow of water into a rotational mechanism, which in turn will transform into electricity with the use of either pump, waterwheel, or turbine. In comparison to solar, geothermal, and wind energy, the use of micro hydroelectricity is quite cheap and easy to build.

# PREPPER'S LONG-TERM SURVIVAL GUIDE

The downside of utilizing this power source is that it will mostly need specific on-site conditions. So, if this is not the restriction around your planned site, then you can prefer it on priority. Micro-hydro energy generation is not very different from wind energy since it uses motion to spin turbines to generate electricity. In this case, the flow of water is the motion that turns the turbines. As long as there is enough water flowing, this method of power generation produces steady electricity. However, the only problem is that investing in this kind of energy generation is costly. It might not be possible to use it for a single household.

## Gas-Powered Generator

All these generators are simple to operate and run on fuel sources readily available for prepping. Aside from just using fuel, such generators are also simple to operate. The primary concern for prepping with a gas-powered generator is that it is inexpensive and accessible to almost all preppers.

However, the size of the generator you choose will be determined by the amount of power you require while out in the wilderness. If you live in a small shelter or cabin, the compact and lightweight versions of gas generators are ideal.

You only need a small amount of power to charge your survival necessities like flashlights, communication devices, extra batteries, and so on.

If you live in a motorhome, you may require the use of a portable generator to meet your energy requirements. Large standby generators can also provide power to homes that are not connected to the main power supply grid. However, using generators for off-grid power can be expensive in the long run. This is the primary reason you should consider the above renewable energy sources.

## Off-Grid Heating

However, your home needs to be heat efficient. When you improve your home's efficiency, you can use all the heat supplied at the same time, reducing your use of energy. If heat energy does not escape from your home, you will not require much of it. If your home is energy efficient, it means that it will retain the heat supplied. This will keep the inside warm for a long period and will minimize the amount of energy you need.

You must also consider the aspect of accessibility to fuel to help you make an informed decision. Ideally, you must consider more than one option to not get stuck when one source fails. This will help you to have a backup source to keep you comfortable when the weather is bad. The following are some of the best off-grid heat sources you must bear in mind.

### Heaters powered by propane

Propane is produced by combining crude oil, gasoline, kerosene, and diesel oil. This type of gas fuel is versatile because it can be used as an off-grid fuel in a variety of appliances including generators, propane space heaters, and cookers. This means that you can use the same fuel source for multiple purposes in your home. If you choose propane, you will not need to obtain additional fuel sources for your heating.

Another benefit of propane heating appliances is the presence of thermostats. A thermostat allows you to control how much energy you use at any given time. This will allow you to save both energy and money. To suit the conditions of the environment, you can adjust the heat to the desired level.

# ENERGY

If the weather is not particularly cold, you may not require additional heat, allowing you to save fuel. Other heating solutions may not allow for this.

### Biomass Energy Systems

Biomass systems are quite complicated, and the results obtained from using them can vary depending on a variety of factors. The amount of biomass you have will determine how much heat you can produce. Biomass is made from waste and resembles a heap of compost. To make biomass, gather all materials that can be naturally degraded by microorganisms.

Compost, leaves, corn, wood chips, and grains are all common materials for this purpose. If you combine these materials, they will generate heat as they degrade. Pipe coils must be strategically placed inside the compost heaps to absorb the heat produced during the biodegradation process. The heat can then be distributed throughout the home. While the solution is useful, you should be aware that it may not be sufficient to heat your entire home. The system has the advantage of being environmentally friendly.

### Heat Exchangers

If you are a homeowner, you should be concerned about using renewable heat sources because they are environmentally friendly. They also do not endanger your health or that of your family. Heat pumps are ideal for off-grid properties due to their numerous advantages. Heat pumps are classified into two types: ground source heat pumps and air source heat pumps.

Air source heat pumps operate on the compression of vapor refrigeration principle. This process assists in absorbing heat from the opposite angle and releasing it to another source. Simply put, this mechanism absorbs heat from an external source and can be used to heat water. This system can extract heat from air at temperatures as low as 20 degrees Fahrenheit. You can use an air source heat pump even in colder climates.

### Wood and fuel

Problems caused by a lack of fuel and a scarcity of wood are becoming more prevalent than ever. Fuel has become scarce or expensive for a variety of reasons, the most important of which are raw materials and transportation costs. The US government is working hard to find multiple solutions, but there are none that are simple. Many prepper blogs have published advice on how to survive this problem, but some believe it will take years before it seriously affects us. Others claim to have a solution to this problem, which is one that most preppers should employ.

You will need to be prepared to survive a crisis. Other supplies will make your prepper life much easier if you have the right gear and supplies. Fuel for your prepping needs is one such item. Because it is not always possible to find fuel during a crisis, it is critical to have backup plans in case gas tanks run dry. When the power goes out, you'll want to have enough fuel to keep your generators or power tools running.

Fuel is just as important as the supplies you put into your prepper bug-out bag. Without a supply of fuel, you won't be able to get out of town and into the wilderness when disaster strikes.

As a prepper, you will have access to all sorts of different sources of fuel to keep you going. Many people may think about just purchasing propane for their home, but that's not going to cut it during any kind of crisis situation. Not only is propane heavy and bulky, but it requires multiple storage cylinders to keep it around for an extended period. It's safest when stored in a locked cabinet or secure garage during bad weather so that no one can steal it from your family's home.

## How to Cook without Power

After a disaster knocks out electricity and gas lines, cooking can be a problem and sometimes even hazardous if you don't stick to a few common sense and basic rules. Let's consider some alternative forms of cooking you can use when you don't have power and still want to prepare a meal.

### Grills, either charcoal or gas

When you don't have power or heat, this is the most obvious way to cook. These, however, should never be used indoors. When you use these indoors, you increase your risk of carbon monoxide asphyxiation as well as your chances of starting a fire that could destroy your home.

### Wood stoves and fireplaces

In many cases, using wood for cooking a meal is an option. If your chimney is in good condition and did not sustain any damage during the disaster, you can cook in it. However, do not light a fire in a fireplace with a broken chimney. Also, make certain that the damper is open. Similarly, if you intend to cook with a wood stove, you must ensure that the stovepipe is not damaged.

### Uncooked Food

This is not to say that you should go out and eat everything raw. This is especially true when it comes to eating fruits, vegetables, and nuts. A fresh salad can be a refreshing alternative to a warm and heavy meal during a power outage in the summer.

### The Solar Grill

This is a newer option that can be pricey. However, it is a fantastic option that allows you to cook your meals using the sun's power. When looking for natural ways to cook, this is an excellent alternative method. However, it is limited by climate, and if you live somewhere that doesn't get a lot of sun, it won't be worth your money.

### Instant or Disposable Grill

This is a less expensive option for an emergency stove to have on hand. This option enables you to prepare a warm meal using a biodegradable option.

### Rocket or Jet Stoves

This is a more recent option. These stoves provide a strong flame as well as the ability to boil water quickly. The main distinction is that jet stoves use gas, whereas rocket stoves use wood.

### Cooking Outside

There are a few things to keep in mind when building a fire and cooking outside:
- Build your fire well away from structures and never in a carport.
- Ensure that all fires are completely extinguished.
- Surround the fire bed with stones or a metal drum.
- A charcoal grill is an excellent place to start a fire.
- Never use gasoline to start a fire, whether it's with wood or charcoal.
- When you're finished, make sure to completely extinguish any fire.

Let us consider some food ideas now that we know how to prepare food without using electricity. Food without power does not imply eating bland packaged or canned food. Consider some of the following delicious meals that you can prepare even when there is no power.

# ENERGY

## Bobcat Cooking Stove

It is an emergency gas stove that is quite useful to have on hand. It runs on cans of ThemaFuel, which allows you to cook inside since it emits no hazardous emissions. A single really can generate a constant flame for roughly four hours and maybe be reused numerous times. Another way to look at it is that solitary can be used to prepare up to 6 emergency meals. This might be an excellent alternative to have in your house in case of an emergency, or it can be used as a portable gas stove for any outdoor excursion.

## Lighting Fire

A crucial survival skill is the ability to start a fire without the use of a lighter or matchsticks. Even if you don't intend to leave society on any road trip, learning how to build a fire by the old-fashioned method is a terrific trick. Here are a few ways to light a fire:

### Use a magnifying lens to light a fire

- All one needs for this method is a lens to focus lighting on a certain location. Both a magnifying glass and a binocular lens are useful.
- Prep the tinder.
- In between the sun and the tinder, place the magnifier. Keep an eye out for the bright dot that emerges. Move the magnifying lens so that the bright dot is about a qtr-inch across and above the tinder.
- For 30-60 seconds, concentrate on the dot. Patience is essential, as it is with other fire-starting procedures. When the tinder begins to smoke, blow softly to spark the flame.

### Light a fire with steel wool and battery

- Only a few batteries and steel wool are required for this method.
- Pull the wool out. It should be around six inches long and at least the size broad.
- Knead the steel wool with the battery. Any battery will work, but 9-volt ones are preferable. Rub the steel against the battery's edges. The wool will begin to glisten and burn.
- To make a bigger fire, place the flaming wool on the tinder stack and blow it gently.

### Use a bow drill to create a fire

- Because it's easier to maintain the pace and weight necessary to generate friction that might spark a fire, the bow drill is probably the best interaction method to utilize. It does, however, require the greatest resources.

## Alternate Light Sources

Oil lamps, candles, kerosene lamps, and mantle lamps: Avoid them. They're a fire hazard. Kerosene Oil lamps give a limited amount of heat and also light. They shine brighter than a candle but are seldom bright enough to read by. To clarify, "lamp oil" is #1-grade kerosene.

If you use these bulbs, you must ventilate. Keep extra wicks in your emergency kit. When putting a lighted bulb anywhere, use caution.

It may become extremely hot above the lamp chimney. Glass is fragile. Metal-framed lamps are safer than glass-framed lamps. Mantles become very brittle when lit and must be replaced on a regular basis.

A mantle lamp emits a great deal of light. Pumping is required to pressurize the liquid fuel tank (white gas). Do not use unleaded fuel in these lanterns unless the lantern is specifically designed for it. Otherwise, the gasoline additives will clog the system.

Camp lamps with screw-in propane canisters are the most practical of these lights. There is no spillage or pumping. Their disadvantage is that they are flammable and perform poorly in cold temperatures.

Light sticks: These provide a lot of cool low-level lighting for a long time. The light is not directed. It can be converted into a flashlight by adding a foil reflector. Headlamps and flashlights: Our flashlights use traditional iridescent bulbs, which waste most of their energy as heat. Fluorescent and LED lighting consumes far less energy. LED bulbs have a lifespan of over 10,000 hours and are shock and cold-resistant. Fluorescent bulbs last ten times as long as iridescent bulbs, but they are dim in cold weather.

LED flashlights with groups of 3 to 8 bulbs will last six times longer than iridescent flashlights with the same batteries. LED lights are now available in various torches and lamps powered by cranks, batteries, or solar panels. Multi-LED touch lights for your home or car start around $10.

# BOOK 7: SECURITY

# PREPPER'S LONG-TERM SURVIVAL GUIDE
## KEEPING SAFE

Securing your home against intruders and looters who may pose a threat if a disaster occurs should be a critical component of your disaster preparation. Disasters can bring out the best in some people while bringing out the worst in others. In the process of protecting our homes, we may also strengthen them against natural forces.

Remember that your first priority should be to protect your family, followed by protecting the money you've earned to provide for your family. We invite you to look over these stages with us and decide which one's sound right for your family in terms of protecting your home from both man's and nature's forces.

Consider other things that will make your home safer and less appealing to approaching humans or animals. Motion-activated lights, for example, are a significant deterrent because they alert the occupants to the intruder and startle animals. Humans are more likely to flee if they believe they will be discovered.

You should inspect your home's entry points for flaws that could lead to an attack. If at all possible, windows should be made of toughened glass or have retractable shutters, and doors should be reinforced. The strength of your structure will be determined by the materials used, but at the very least, ensure that all entry points, including windows, can be closed and locked. Even a weak lock is preferable to no lock.

If you have access to power, a good alarm system is also a plus, though you can build a makeshift alarm system by hanging things like cans and wind chimes in common walkways.

Always begin your home defense planning by considering what intruders you might face and how they might approach you. Prepare not only for humans but also for the animals you may encounter. You should have a warning system and a strategy in place to deal with as many different scenarios as possible.

Long-term survival situations necessitate a high level of security and defense. You'll get nothing out of having a year's worth of food and water if you can get rid of it. It's also worth noting that most of today's typical domestic security systems are designed to alert authorities in the event of an intruder or other emergency. A police officer is called to the house due to the sound of a window shattering. When things are going well, the strategy is usually effective. In times of crisis, however, dialing 911 will be obsolete. Most people fantasize about driving down the road with their headlights on and sirens blaring. You are the only one who knows what happened to your window when it was broken at 2:00 a.m. Many factors should be included in your security strategy, such as defensive weaponry, structural hardening, alarm systems, and, most importantly, situational awareness. But first, let's go over the fundamentals.

**Security Lighting and Alarms**

Intruders hate bright lights because they may impede them from concealing themselves in the gloom or shadows.

Add outside lighting to highlight entrances and windows. Install motion-sensitive security lights in key spots that will turn on when there is movement but will stay off the rest of the night.

# SECURITY

Install motion-sensor nightlights around your house. They illuminate your route through dark corridors at night and turn on automatically when someone walks by. It may discreetly warn you of an attacker's presence in your house.

The faster you detect an intruder, the greater chances you have of neutralizing the threat or reacting effectively. Alarm systems are, therefore extremely important. They could be as simple as a system of strings linked to bells or tin cans containing pebbles. Once the intruder touches one of the strings, it will make a sound and alert you.

You can opt for something less primitive and get some battery-powered alarms, such as motion sensors, however, make sure you have enough batteries to use them through long periods in a survival situation, at least a few months' worth of batteries. If you do use battery-powered motion sensors, do your research and find out the best locations for them around your perimeter.

Equally as effective as installing cameras will be to install lighting systems. Burglars and intruders will do everything they can to keep themselves concealed while trying to enter your home, but lights will ensure they cannot do so.

You can also install lights both outside your home and inside. Motion sensor lighting systems work great outside your homes, such as at your entrances, patio, garage, and front lawn. Solar-powered lights, in particular, will be the least expensive option.

For indoor lighting, use a light timer such as the kind that you use during Christmas, and keep it connected to your lamp. This will also create the illusion that you are home.

Other deterrents include sounds or noises, which may dissuade a would-be robber while also alerting neighbors to suspicious activity.

Security alarms employ sound to disorient attackers, dissuade them, and notify them that a place has been violated.

When you leave the house, leave a television or radio on to create the idea that someone is home. Barking dog alarms employ microwave and radar technologies to detect activity outside a door. Some make a German shepherd-like sound, and the barking grows more fierce as the action continues.

Motion sensors in the driveway or outdoor areas will sound an alert if someone enters the monitoring area. Look around for a range of security devices that employ sound to give an extra layer of safety.

These systems are a great way to add an extra layer of security to your home. An alarm system may give an intruder a few seconds' notice and shock him. Monitored alarm systems notify the alarm company, which contacts local law enforcement.

The real reaction time may be rather sluggish. Alarms will not discourage a determined intruder from breaking into your house. When the electricity is off, system batteries may rapidly deplete.

It is better not to rely on an alarm system to protect you during a prolonged power loss until you have a backup power source.

**Watch Dogs**

A barking dog may be a good alarm for one and one family to be aware of and keep safe from any dangers since many burglaries occur when the house residents are present. It is also a fantastic deterrent, and even something as easy as placing a sign that says "Beware of the Dog" will make potential burglars think twice about choosing one house as their next target.

This is a simple home security hack that many people take already. There's a good reason why: a dog is a much more effective home defensive measure than you're probably willing to give it credit for.

First and foremost, if you get a dog, it's probably to give your family a companion you can love and cherish. Purchasing a dog to serve as a guard dog is probably a secondary reason to own one for you.

The mere presence of a dog or the sound of one barking is sufficient to send many criminals out of your house or even out of your property in the first place.

In addition, a larger dog, such as a German Shepherd, could defend you by keeping you safe from an intruder once they've entered your home or general premises.

But by far, the biggest reason to have a guard dog is the fact that they are simply one of the best alarm systems available. The moment a dog senses danger, it will bark out loud and rush to the site of danger.

Having at least two guard dogs will be even better than less one. Yes, it's more mouths to feed, but it will be more intimidating to intruders.

While a larger dog will always be better for home defense, if you have small dogs, they will at least be able to alert you to danger. Smaller dogs tend to be more alert than larger ones, and the very sound of them barking may be enough to send an intruder scurrying as well.

Having one or more dogs is a great way to keep yourself safe while in the wilderness, especially if you choose large canine companions. A dog's senses are far sharper than a person's, so your dog may alert you to danger before you detect it yourself. A dog is also a great deterrent against people and many other animals, and dogs are fiercely protective of their owners. They will alert you to someone approaching your home or danger out in the brush, and they are powerful fighters.

A dog may also be able to assist you in:
- Detecting intruders
- Frightening intruders
- Avoiding nearby animals
- Hunting and finding food
- Alerting you to nearby danger
- Fighting off animals/intruders in extreme circumstances

Some people also use "Beware of dog" signs even if they don't have a dog — while this won't be effective against everyone, it may be enough to encourage some intruders to pause or choose another location.

Of course, having dogs does bring some additional responsibilities and advantages; you must feed, care for, and protect your animals just as they protect you. You will need a reliable source of food and water for them, the ability to keep them warm, and the ability to keep them safe. You must make sure you control the dog when something unexpected happens so it doesn't attack something dangerous and get hurt or escalate a situation you might otherwise be able to walk away from. Teach your faultless dog to recall to get it away from other animals, or it may prove a liability and an asset.

# SECURITY

**Protect Your Garage**

Most people who are serious about home security understand the importance of fortifying their doors and windows, but far fewer understand the importance of fortifying their garage.

Many homes have been broken into because intruders entered through the garage rather than the doors or windows. You don't want to make the same mistake of leaving your garage open to the elements. Don't ignore it.

Keep in mind that burglars may choose your garage over the rest of your house because they know most garages contain valuable items such as tools, important financial documents, and, of course, your car. And if they do decide to enter the rest of your house, they'll have an easy way in.

You can protect your garage by doing the following:
- Replacing your current garage door with a heavy-duty door
- Replacing the door leading from your garage into your home with a steel door, and heavy-duty locks.
- Keep any precious possessions out of the garage and other belongings in it hidden.
- Install a motion sensor light.
- Install security cameras (even if they are fake).
- Never leave your keys or any other valuable possessions in your vehicle.

**Use Locks Everywhere in Your House**

Keeping locks on your doors and windows and all other exit points leading outside is great, but at the same time, you don't want to neglect to keep things locked in your home.

Your home more than likely has precious items within it, and you need to keep those protected. Examples of items that you need to give extra security include electronics, firearms and ammunition, jewelry, personal documents, items of personal value, and any survival stockpiles you have made (food, water, etc.) One of the best defensive measures is keeping your valuables in a safe with a durable lock bolted to the floor. Many times, burglars will take the whole safe with them if they can't break into it.

Lock your jewelry boxes and any other important boxes as well. You obviously won't be able to lock your TV, so that's one risk you may have to take.

**The fundamentals of reinforcing doors**

Before we begin, here are some fundamentals of door reinforcement:

Deadbolts are the industry standard, and all exterior doors should have one. Small, ineffective locks built into door knobs can be defeated in about 3 seconds with a credit card.

Invest in high-quality locks; cheap locks can be quickly, quietly, and easily picked or bumped. Purchase the strongest door available. Windows that allow access to the door's locking mechanism are harmful and defeat the purpose of strengthening your door. A broken window allows an intruder easy access to the inside of your home. If possible, remove the window or cover it with decorative anti-theft bars or security film. Have a way to check the door without opening it. Hinges/bolts should be on the inside, otherwise an intruder can pull them out and disassemble the door.

The front door of the average home is secured with a deadbolt. While deadbolts are desirable, they should be reinforced to withstand a concentrated entry attempt. All that stands between you and a thug attempting to break down your door is the doorframe, which is typically only an inch or two of wood thick. Typically, that wood gives way in a common kicking attack. After a couple of kicks, the guys in the back are in.

**Hiding Places**

Properties that have lots of natural hiding places, such as trees, brush, shrubbery, and so on, are a magnet for burglars because they know they can conceal themselves. Even homes with lots of outside shadows will be appealing to burglars.

Does this rule out having natural foliage on your property? No, but it does imply that you should keep them as neat and trim as possible to reduce the number of hiding places for a burglar.

It is much easier to include all of the necessary functionality when you start from scratch. However, many essentials can be added to an existing room, so don't rule out using this option entirely. Consider the number of people your safe space is intended to accommodate when determining the appropriate size. It is recommended that you provide at least 5 square feet of floor area per person when dealing with a short-term emergency, such as a tornado. It's worth noting that I mentioned square feet of floor area rather than total room size.

As we'll see later, you'll want to keep a few supplies in the safe room, so make sure you have enough room for them.

The bare minimum is five square feet per person, and if you intend to stay in the safe room for more than an hour or two, that area will need to be significantly expanded. It is recommended that you plan on working at least twenty-four hours per day. Each person will require at least 7 or 8 square feet. Why? As a result, you and your family will have enough space to sleep comfortably. So, if you have a family of five and want to stay in the safe room for up to three days, you'll need at least 35 to 40 square feet of floor space, not including the space required by your supplies.

Even though you want to keep comfort in mind, you don't intend to use the safe room as a weekend retreat. When additional space for equipment and supplies is taken into account, a family of five could easily make do with a 7-foot-square room. In general, the basement is the best location for a safe room in most situations. Placing it in this location provides excellent protection from Mother Nature's wrath. That is, assuming your property was not built in a flood-prone area. If this is the case, you should raise the bar slightly higher. The disadvantage is that if you intend to use the safe room to defend against a bandit horde, a cellar is probably not the best location.

The only way around this is to prepare ahead and make provisions for some type of last-ditch escape path. I would not recommend digging any kind of underground tunnel unless you are sustained that you know what you're doing. If you don't, you may as well be constructing nothing more than a mass cemetery.

**Use Warning Signs**

You've likely driven by homes or properties before with signs outside such as "KEEP OUT!" or "BEWARE OF GUARD DOG!"

There's a good reason why you commonly see these signs; they are actually effective at keeping burglars (particularly less experienced ones) at bay. The reason why is that it tells them that you are someone who is taking the defense of your property and home very seriously.

If you're still not convinced that setting up warning signs is effective, just know that it is believed warning signs reduce the chances of having your home broken into by over fifty percent.

# SECURITY

## Perimeter Defense

Making a perimeter defense is one of the most effective ways to secure your home and may deter animals and people. Perimeter defense will typically take the form of a fence, but you can also use plants, rocks, or other materials to make approaching your home more difficult.

You can construct your perimeter defense using natural resources or buy and erect fencing.

You can also scatter holly leaves, old bramble, thistles, and other sharp, spiky materials around. However, keep pathways clear so that you can easily enter and exit your home. While closing off all routes may appear valuable, it may trap you near your home, which may not be very safe.

If you run out of spiky materials, you can make dead hedges out of cutting wood. This is simple to make; simply weave together old sticks, branches, and dead plants to create an impenetrable mesh. Even if someone or something does break through, they will almost certainly make a lot of noise to alert you to their presence.

You should not create a perimeter defense designed to injure someone who is approaching. It is unsafe and illegal in many states, so doing so could get you into trouble with the law, especially if it hurts someone. Digging and concealing pits, creating tripwires, or otherwise rigging the environment to make it unsafe for someone approaching is dangerous and illegal and should be avoided. Booby traps are not the solution to keeping your home safe.

## Early Warning Systems

An early warning system is also a great idea; it will alert you to animals or people coming near the house. Start by working out how far you want your early warning system to be from your home. You need to hear it when it sounds clear, but it should be far enough that you get a good amount of warning when someone is approaching. You may find that it helps to talk to other party members and agree upon a distance together.

Early warning systems usually rely on audible or visual alerts, which will give you a sense of which direction the intruder is approaching. They may involve triggering a light or an alarm, which will tell you that someone is coming. An audible system may be more effective if you need it to wake you up and might also be better for frightening off animals.

LED motion lights, if bright enough, can easily deter both animals and people by startling them. If even that isn't an option, you can still create a basic early warning system by hanging up or balancing items that will make a noise when disturbed.

Many people use tin cans suspended on a wire, with the cans dangling at around head height (so the wire is not a hazard). Fill the cans with stones. Someone approaching the house will disturb the cans, creating a clattering noise that alerts you to their approach. Balancing rocks near pathways can also work, although this may make less noise and needs to be reset each time disturbed.

Make sure your early warning system is tricky enough to trigger that it won't constantly be disturbed by the wind or by your own group members coming and going, or you may find that you stop responding to it as you should. Ideally, it should only be set off by someone's unexpected approach, although this may not be possible with some motion-triggered devices.

## Traps and Funneling

Because of the time and effort required, transforming your garden into a giant trap is not a viable option, especially if you have a large garden. Furthermore, any visit to your garden could be fatal.

Instead, use traps strategically to direct intruders to an area that you can easily defend, a technique known as funneling. This usually entails forcing intruders to reveal themselves and not allowing them to remain hidden. If an intruder wants to get from the garden gates to your front door, they will take the most direct route possible: a straight line. In that case, you'd want to have debris or anything else that would cause them to deviate from that path and onto the path of the traps you've set up.

Avoid placing random traps around your home can also be dangerous to you and legitimate visitors, especially after dark. Don't, however, dismiss the subject entirely.

Funneling is a hunting technique that involves pushing the prey into the right area so that it can be caught. Although intruders are not treated as prey, a similar principle applies here. Instead, you're attempting to drive them into open areas where they're more likely to be noticed and less likely to hang out.

To set up this arrangement, carefully survey your home's area and assess the various spaces. Where would you hide if you were trying to sneak around? What bushes, structures, and debris might offer refuge? What could you possibly hide beneath?

You want to push intruders away from these areas, forcing them to stay on the pathway or in the open. You can funnel an intruder into open spaces by making the other spaces difficult to pass through. For example, piling up boxes or old tools in hideaways or along the edges of paths discourages intruders from entering these areas. If they try it, they are also more likely to make a noise and alert you.

**Windows Security Is a Must-Have**

In most cases, windows do not serve as a deterrent to intruders. Any parent who has a child who enjoys baseball understands how simple it is to shatter a window while the child is playing. This can be reduced to a minimum if the glass is replaced with shatter-resistant plastic. It is available under a variety of brand names, including Lexan, and is strong enough to withstand hammer strikes. Alternatively, depending on your preferences, you can buy it in sheets and cut it to size with a circular saw fitted with a plywood finishing blade or a jigsaw fitted with a metal cutting blade. To avoid chipping, keep your speed low. An intruder will be forced to find another way to open the window if they are unable to smash through the glass. Fortunately, this can be avoided by drilling a hole in the window sashes and inserting a small, inconspicuous nail into the hole. The hole should extend at least 12 inches through the bottom rail of the top sash.

You want the spot to be slightly larger than the nail so that you can simply spine the pin when you need to open the window. Make sure the gap is angled downward, so the nail does not fall out on its own. Repeat this procedure twice for each window, leaving about 2 inches on each side of the window. As previously stated, horizontal sliding windows, like sliding doors, can be locked.

Casement windows are difficult to open from the outside, but they are functional. If you want to increase security, you can install special latches that require a key to open. Assume you're putting in any of these numerous steps to secure your windows. In that case, it is critical that you not only limit outside entry but also potentially seal yourself and your family inside in the event of a fire. If you're considering installing permanent security measures, such as the window grilles we'll discuss next, consider how important it is to be able to evacuate quickly in the event of an emergency.

# SECURITY

Although they are not the most attractive things globally, bars over windows will almost likely prevent most attackers from entering. Although they are pretty simple to install, they might be challenging for the typical individual. The grilles should be secured to the wall using the most vital area of the wall that is accessible. If feasible, avoid using wood screws and use sturdy lag bolts instead. Once the grille is in place, return to the lag bolts and use a handheld grinder to round off the heads, making them almost hard to remove once they have been placed. To avoid using wood screws, grind the screw heads down until they are no longer accessible to a screwdriver's point of contact with the screw head.

## Walls Provide Protection

The walls of most stick-built houses are not particularly difficult to break, even though doors and windows may offer accessible entry points for intruders. If the home has siding over the pressboard, it would take a few minutes with a chainsaw or even a sledgehammer to construct a new door.

Although this is the case, it would take a determined invader to proceed down that path. The majority of individuals have been trained to concentrate on doors and windows to obtain admission. If you have a large enough budget, brick exterior walls will significantly boost wall strength. On the other hand, an invader with a sledgehammer may even be the most sophisticated of defenses. Interior walls in most houses provide little to no protection against weapons in most situations. Remember what we mentioned about covering one's tracks vs. concealing one's tracks? However, inside walls give excellent hiding, but no cover; sandbags and other heavy materials placed in strategic locations may increase the cover factor.

## Nighttime Security

Nighttime security when you are off the grid can be challenging if you don't have electricity because you will usually operate in the dark. You should always have emergency lighting of some sort, even if it's just a flashlight that can be hand-cranked.

If possible, use battery-powered motion sensor lights around your home, so you know that you will never be operating entirely in the dark; This can help you when you need to leave the house at night and deter intruders.

Practice a nighttime routine of locking doors and windows, just as you would in an ordinary home, and make sure you secure outside areas such as sheds and gates if necessary.

## Fire Safety

It is critical to be aware of the dangers that fire poses, especially at night. Fires should always be extinguished or left with very low flames, protected by proper fireguards, and with no fuel nearby. Keep flammable materials away from the area around a fire.

Make sure your home has smoke detectors and carbon monoxide alarms and that they are working properly. You should also keep a fire extinguisher in an easily accessible location in your home.

Outside, fire safety should be prioritized. Put out a fire before leaving it unattended so that sparks do not fly and catch on nearby brush. Have water tanks on hand to put out stray fires; these can be outfitted with a pump and a hose to serve as your fire-fighting kit. Tanks should be placed as high uphill as possible so that gravity can help the pump.

However, prevention is always preferable to cure. Use a good fire guard and keep any flammables away from the area around a fire pit. Never leave a fire unattended, especially in windy conditions. Prepare several buckets of non-flammable material, such as soil or sand, to throw on the flames if they spread. If there is no water available, these can be used in an emergency to help put out any spreading fires.

**Defensive Weapons**

Assuming that you don't have one already, you should have at least one gun in your home that's made for home defense. Maybe you were passed down firearms from a parent or grandparent, but if those firearms are not suitable models for home defense, then you will need to buy a separate one.

The best home defense weapons will be a pump-action shotgun in 12 gauge or 20 gauge, a handgun with a minimum chambering of .38 Special or 9mm Luger, or a semi-automatic defensive rifle such as an AR-15 or AK-47.

Regardless of which home defense gun you choose, it's important that you keep it as secure as possible and within easy access of you. Installing a handgun safe on your bed with fingerprint identification is the safest option to go with. You can quickly access the gun inside with a simple print identification, it's by you while you're sleeping, and your children won't be able to get into it.

Humans have been using weapons to defend themselves since the very beginning. Weapons come in many forms, some are designed to attack, others to defend, but most are versatile and their purpose depends on the wielder. For most of us, just the thought of holding a firearm, for example, is petrifying, never mind injuring someone with it, however, there are many people that would shoot without thinking twice. This already happens, imagine what would happen if a catastrophe hit when society's common sense no longer prevails.

You may think that a baseball bat or any other short-range weapon will suffice for defense, but chances are that they won't do much to protect you against a firearm. If you want to be truly prepared, then you should get your hands on a long-distance weapon. You don't need to go out there and get a sniper, but a handgun, or something more discreet that you can take with you when you go outside to do chores, would probably be a better choice.

Of course, the best type of defense weapon depends on the user. Every gun owner has different preferences; we will go over the various types of guns so you can make an informed decision. But, before we get there, it's important to discuss the decision of when, if ever, to shoot. This is a very difficult decision to make; in fact, there are no guidelines on this subject, and it is entirely dependent on the circumstances. However, some pointers may be useful if the situation arises. First, determine your goal. Avoid pulling the trigger in low-light situations or when under intense stress because the mind can play many tricks in those situations. Always know who or what you're going to shoot at, but also what's behind the target; you don't want to shoot or hit the wrong person. Another thing to consider when using a gun is that just because there is no rule of law at the time does not mean you should act lawlessly. Shoot only when absolutely necessary, and keep in mind that the law may be restored one day, and authorities may investigate crimes committed during those times of crisis. Finally, if you and your family or group are well and safe at the end of a confrontation, you have most likely made the right decision.

# SECURITY

Non-firearm weapons will be rendered ineffective against firearms. They can, however, be useful as tools. When shopping for knives, look for a blade that is 5 to 6 inches long and has a full tang. This means that the knife's blade extends all the way through the handle, increasing its stability. The blade's thickness is also important; the thicker the blade, the less likely it is to break.

## Situational Awareness

You should always be alert to what's happening in your local vicinity and whether it presents any dangers to you or others.

You should practice being aware of your surroundings whenever possible, especially if you are in a new area with unknown threats. For example, if you are in an area where you may encounter dangerous animals, you should be cautious and watch for signs of what you may be dealing with.

Animal tracks, droppings, and environmental damage should all help you determine what is likely to be in the area. You may also pick up scents for specific animals. If there are other people in the area, you may discover evidence of fires, dwellings, or debris (e.g., litter).

It's not easy to develop situational awareness, but you can start by not listening to music while you're out and about and by changing up your routine on a regular basis, so you don't operate on autopilot.

According to some, situational awareness entails perception, comprehension, and projection. Here's an example:

You're exploring a new neighborhood. Using your perception, you assess the surrounding environment and notice a pile of feathers under a bush. Your understanding of the situation leads you to believe that a predator is nearby, but the bird is small, and the only predators in this area hunt at night. You project that it is safe to continue walking, but keep an eye out for fresh tracks and ensure you have a weapon handy.

Situational awareness entails gathering information, analyzing it, and acting on it. Making this your default operating mode could save your life.

You should also work on this as a group effort, involving others in your group. Practice identifying common threat signs and discussing how you would handle any dangers that may arise as a result of them. This group activity is an excellent way to raise both collective and individual awareness.

This is a growing problem in today's society. Too many people are burying their faces in their phones, completely unaware of their surroundings. This is the polar opposite of what you want in a survival situation. In fact, you want to know when and where someone is likely to approach your home. You want to be hyper-aware of everything around you.

If anyone approaches your perimeter, they should be challenged, but you don't want to start shooting right away. Before taking any further action, use diplomacy and ask questions. Another thing to keep in mind, especially if someone approaches your home, is that they could be a distraction. In other words, they could be diverting your attention away from someone else approaching your perimeter from another direction. Ideally, your group would have enough people to rotate surveillance so that you are always aware of what is going on within your perimeter.

If you don't have enough people in your group to take shifts and rotate, then you should consider getting a dog. Besides being great companions, a well-trained dog can do the job of several people when it comes to detecting intruders.

### Keep Doors and Windows locked

This may seem obvious, but a locking mechanism is useless if not utilized. There's no level of extra protection that can compensate for the importance of securing your windows and doors. Encourage members of the family to keep the home secured tight on a regular basis. Locking all ports of access makes it more difficult for an attacker to enter the residence, giving it a more challenging target. Keep records of your house keys. If keys have been lost long enough for everyone to manufacture a duplicate of it, rekey all locks. Never put a spare key beneath the mat or plant pot, just above the door frame, in a phony rock beside the front entrance, or even on a window sill. Consider the following position if you need to conceal a key.

- Safely tucked up within a mean-looking dog home.
- Buried inside a side yard, inside the short PVC pipe with both ends sealed.
- Within a properly fitted, coded lockbox that is situated out of sight.

To give access to your house to family members, you may wish to change certain keys entirely and install a UL Deadbolt on a backdoor. It functions similarly to a garage code.

If your kid misplaces a key, you must rekey all the doors in your house. If he inadvertently reveals the password, all you've to do is reprogram it. It also provides the added security of rewriting the code on a regular basis to ensure that this has not been hacked.

### Landscape

Trespassers may be drawn or discouraged by the terrain itself. Landscape design can provide a beautiful setting while also protecting your property. If done correctly, it can be almost as effective as a cutting barbed wire security barriers without drawing attention or appearing menacing.

- Make it difficult for trespassers to hide in your terrain.
- Keep any plants or shrubs that could be used as a hiding place away from doors and windows.
- Keep large tree branches away from the house to prevent entry through second-story windows.
- Keep hedges in front of the house trimmed to less than 3 feet tall to avoid creating a screen behind which anyone can hide.

A lawn with tall grass indicates to a burglar that either A. your home is possibly unoccupied, or B. you aren't taking home security seriously.

Besides, you shouldn't have tall grass on your lawn in the first place because it looks bad. If you're planning on going away on a long trip or vacation, you can hire a teenager in your neighborhood to help keep your lawn cut. It will do more than you may think it will be at making a burglar think twice about intruding.

# BOOK 8: HEALTH

# PREPPER'S LONG-TERM SURVIVAL GUIDE
## CHAPTER 1: THE PREPPER'S INFIRMARY

If you have the knowledge but not the supplies and tools, treating anything will be quite hard. It is best to start collecting the supplies to treat the most common injuries, such as contusions or lacerations. Any little scratch or open wound has to be treated immediately, or it might cause infections. One of the main issues of living in such a medically advanced world is our weakened immune systems — even the healthiest of people nowadays have weaker immune systems when compared to our ancestors that lived centuries ago.

Even mundane activities such as cutting firewood can cause strains and sprains in your muscles, especially for those that are not used to it. Any open wound can become a huge issue if not treated properly and promptly. Digestive issues can also become common as we adapt to the new diet. Because all communications will mostly be done in person, contagious diseases such as viruses can also spread more easily.

There will be a lot more dangers than you might anticipate once you remove all the medical care that we are used to today. To combat that, you should stock as much medicine for these diseases and injuries as you possibly can.

# HEALTH

**Medical Emergency Survival Guide**

Panic can be as harmful to our health as the underlying conditions. With the recent increase in medical emergencies and the ever-increasing complexity of healthcare, having a plan has never been more important.

It's not something we ever want to think about, but it's always a possibility. Being prepared for a medical emergency can be the difference between life and death. Today, we're going to talk about what you can do to improve your chances of surviving a medical emergency. Let's get started!

Remember to breathe: This may seem obvious, but people can hyperventilate and pass out. Stay calm — being unsure or worried only widens your stress response system, which will deplete more energy from your body faster than it normally would during an emergency. Take deep breaths while you attempt to assess the situation, and don't forget to think clearly!

Remember your ABCs: Any minor injuries (such as cuts or bruises) should be cleaned and exposed to fresh air. Cover them with a clean cloth, lightly pat them to help the clotting process, and check for signs of infection. Apply pressure to the wound to slow blood flow until the bleeding stops. Lift any nearby objects from the ground and place them beneath the wound if there is a lot of blood—this will help slow blood flow.

Knowing about any medical conditions you have can be useful in the event of a medical emergency. Keep your medications, allergies, and doctor list on hand, and keep your information up to date.

If you have valuables, consider storing them in home safes, a bank safe deposit box, or at a friend's house. If someone asks to look at your valuables, simply say, "I'm sorry, but I don't have time to let you rummage through everything we own." What time is it now? Do you know where I can find my glasses?

If you have been injured, try to keep a clear head and assess the severity of your injuries. Try to stay calm—panicking will only make you feel worse, and it's more likely that you'll injure yourself further.

If you have been severely injured and clean sheets and blankets, consider using them to help stem the bleeding. Make sure that they are alcohol-free, though, because rubbing alcohol can cause more damage.

When trying to treat an injury on your own, remember that every situation is different depending on what type of injury it is. If you're injured, it's important to stay still and as comfortable as possible. If you are injured, make sure that you're treating the injuries appropriately.

Once an injury has been treated, try packing the wound to prevent further contamination or infection. By plugging the damage, you're effectively stopping any water from entering the wound. If you leave the wound open, water can enter and cause an infection to grow in there. This could then lead to secondary infections and further damage.

If you should be injured while transported in a vehicle, get out immediately when it's safe to do so (if that's possible). If possible, try to sit up or move away from the vehicle as quickly as possible while still moving. This is similar to the old saying about stopping, then stepping away from a car after an accident. Depending on what you were injured by, it could be more beneficial to sit up or move away from the vehicle, but you need to use your judgment in that situation. And if you're in a medical emergency, then you should grab your kit and be prepared to treat yourself or your patient.

# PREPPER'S LONG-TERM SURVIVAL GUIDE

Medical supplies and equipment are vital in emergency situations. However, when a crisis happens, it is possible that the medical supply stockpiles will not last long enough to aid everyone. When these scenarios arise, some people who have more advanced medical knowledge may be able to help by writing out a list of necessary supplies and distributing them where they are needed. This part will cover what medical supplies and equipment should be included in an emergency stockpile for different populations and the importance of having an inventory system that can track the usage of items so that they can be replaced before it is too late.

Medical supplies and equipment are crucial in emergency situations. When plagues or diseases occur, many people will be affected by them. This means that medical supplies and equipment are needed in a lot of different places. The most essential medical supplies used during a crisis would include gravity-defying antibiotic pills and small first-aid kits designed with the specific needs of the affected population in mind. Some other useful items would include food, water, sanitation products, batteries, flashlights, batteries, and other small items such as nail clippers or sewing kits that can be used to fix clothes when they have been torn or soiled during an emergency event.

A lot of medical supplies and equipment can be stored in a well-organized and secure location. When one is preparing for a crisis, it is critical to have a good storage plan that will keep medical supplies safe. The best way to safeguard these supplies would be to build them and store them in large closets or storage areas that locks have secured. These caches could be built in neatly organized rooms like basements and should include the necessary information about how much of each supply is present and where these items are kept. If they are not available when they are needed, having a good supply system can make it easier to distribute the necessary supplies when a catastrophe strikes.

When preparing for a crisis, it is important to understand the populations that may need more medical supplies than others. It is generally agreed that older people have a harder time recovering from injuries because of slower healing times and other issues. Other populations who may need extra medical supplies include children, pregnant women, and people who have been injured during an emergency event. The best way to take care of these populations would be to use extra gravity-defying antibiotic pills and provide them with emergency first-aid kits. All these supplies should be given out along with safe food and water rations too.

It is also essential that people know and understand the importance of having an inventory system so that medical supplies can be replaced. An inventory system for medical supplies and equipment is critical to track their usage. When this information is collected, it becomes easier to replace items before they run out of use entirely. This means that a good primary care physician may have to know how many antibiotics are being distributed and dispensed so that they can order more in time if these supplies get low. A good inventory database should include barcode scanning systems, which make it easier to track the usage of these supplies as time passes by.

Many of these items that seem like large stockpiles may actually only be enough for a few people at once. When planning out your stockpile, instead of neglecting your medical supply needs, you should remember that the important thing is to have these resources ready whenever they are needed and not worry about having them on hand every single day.

# HEALTH

## Survival First-Aid Kit

In the event of an emergency, it's best to be prepared. That way, you won't have to carry a heavy bag of essentials or spend valuable time digging through drawers and closets trying to find anything that could be used. Also, keep in mind that if you are outdoors, you will need items like a knife, sunscreen, bug spray, a raincoat, and waterproof matches for emergencies.

A good kit should include bandages and first-aid items for cuts and scrapes, tweezers for removing splinters (and ticks), a thermometer, pain relievers, antiseptic towelettes, and anything else you think you might need. Don't forget to pack extra medication that you take daily. It is also important to pack non-perishable food items in case you need sustenance quickly.

Make sure the kit is properly stored in an easy-to-carry container. If possible, store it where you can grab it, and go in an emergency, such as right by the front door or near the bedside table.

A well-stocked first-aid kit can be the difference between life and death. In a survival situation, an injured person may have to wait hours or days for help—and with a severe injury, you may not have any help at all. You want your first-aid kit to give you the best chance of successfully treating injuries and illnesses.

With an adequate supply of medicines, bandages, and sterilizing tools, you can take care of yourself and help those around you when you don't have access to medical facilities. Don't go by what you see in first aid kits in local stores.

## Items to Include in an Emergency Kit

Include the following items:

### Sutures and Sterilizing Substances

Sutures are not required in most emergencies, but they should be included if space is available in your kit. They are used to stop internal bleeding as well as to close cuts and lacerations. Use dental floss for a thread because it is strong and already waxed at the ends. Before stitching incisions together, an alcohol-based antiseptic can be used to disinfect the wound from bacteria and other germs.

Tape can be used to keep sutures in place, but duct tape is more practical, especially if you have a larger wound. Buy Steri-Strips instead of traditional butterfly bandages because they seal wounds better and heal faster. If you have a Mylar blanket or another metallic or reflective material, you can use it to reflect sunlight on the damage to speed up the healing process.

To prevent infection, antibiotic ointments such as Neosporin can be applied to wounds. Chlorhexidine antiseptic should also be included because it prevents disease and bacteria from spreading beneath the stitches or bandaging.

### Infection Prevention

Before touching any wounds, use antibacterial hand wipes to disinfect your hands. Avoid using public restrooms if you don't want to spread bacteria and get sick. You can also use hand sanitizer gel or spray before touching anything.

A total body cleansing station equipped with lancets, alcohol swabs, alcohol wipes, a thermometer for checking body temperature, and a thermometer tape measure would be ideal for assisting with wound care.

A portable foot bath can be used to disinfect and clean wounds on the feet. It is suitable for cleaning, but it lacks antibacterial properties, so the damage will remain infected.

Any medical tape or bandage that has been approved by the FDA may be used. Please ensure that they are latex-free and suitable for use on human skin or wounds. You may also want to select a specific brand of medical tape because some may contain silicone, a substance that can cause skin irritation or burning, especially if you don't notice it right away.

### Splints, bandages, and slings

A home or car emergency kit is a must-have. But remember to replenish your supplies at least once a year!

Many people believe that sterile gauze, bandages, slings, and splints are only used in emergencies. These commonplace items, however, should be included in an emergency kit. They can also be used in the medical field as part of a daily routine.

Bandages can limit swelling and stop bleeding by absorbing blood after an injury to the area where they are applied. Slings help immobilize an injured limb while taking pressure off the injured joint or spine nearby. Splints can help stabilize a broken limb or broken bone until it is healing or has been set.

## First-Aid Tips in Different Emergency Situations

A first-aid kit is an excellent tool to have on hand, but it's not always the best solution. That's because there are many types and degrees of emergencies, from minor scrapes and sprains to life-threatening accidents and disasters. In some cases, you need more than just first aid; you may also need to evacuate!

## Incident of choking

If someone chokes on something, first ask them what they are blocking, and then try the Heimlich maneuver to remove the object from their airway.

## Shock treatment

It can cause serious complications, so it must be treated as soon as possible. Take a blood pressure reading if someone is in shock. If their blood pressure is low, start giving them warm liquids intravenously. Then, try to keep the patient as calm as possible to avoid a seizure or cardiac arrest.

This could save the life of a friend you're exploring with. Shock, which occurs after a traumatic event, such as a near-drowning or a serious injury, such as breaking a bone, can be lethal in the wilderness. Recognizing shock symptoms allows you to observe them and treat the person by keeping them calm, keeping them warm or cool to maintain their body temperature, or elevating their feet.

## Stemming bleeding

It is critical to be able to stop or control bleeding while out in the wilderness. If large wounds or arterial bleeding are not controlled, they can result in death. Bright red blood indicates arterial bleeding. Learning how to apply pressure to slow or stop bleeding and how to properly bandage a wound will help them avoid losing too much blood. In the event of severe bleeding, a tourniquet should be used as a last resort because the improper application can result in complications or limb loss.

# HEALTH

## Cuts and scrapes

The first thing you should do if someone is bleeding is to keep them from losing too much blood. Locate a bandage or clean cloth as soon as possible and apply it liberally to the wound. Apply the bandage to the wound and check to see if the bleeding has stopped after 20 to 30 minutes. If this occurs, clean the wound with a damp towel and an antiseptic. Do not apply soap to open wounds. Apply an antibiotic spray to the wound and cover it with a bandage. Never apply a spray or ointment to a cut that appears to be too deep or isn't stopping the bleeding. Cover it loosely with a towel to prevent infection. For a simple nosebleed, simply lean slightly forward and press a tissue or cloth against the person's nostrils until the bleeding stops.

## Sprains and fractures

It may be difficult to distinguish between sprains and fractures. If the body part appears strange, cannot be moved, or screams for several hours, it is most likely a broken bone rather than a simple sprain. Sprains usually heal on their own, but there are ways to speed up the healing process. This can be accomplished by applying ice to the skin, which constricts blood vessels and decreases blood flow. Wrap the icing bag in a towel to prevent it from coming into contact with sensitive skin. Ice the injury for a few minutes, then rest for a few minutes before repeating the ice. Maintain the elevation of the area and avoid putting any weight on it. A splint may be used to stabilize and prevent the bones from moving if you suspect someone has broken bones. Avoid straightening the bones because it may cause more harm than good. Apply an ice pack to the injured area and give the person pain relievers to help with swelling.

## Lightning strikes caused medical condition

Lightning strikes can also be a problem when prepping in the wild because the preppers are usually exposed. As a result, you must ensure that you are taking the necessary precautions, such as not moving during storms. Loss of consciousness, paralysis, seizures, and blast trauma, including broken bones and eardrum ruptures, can all be caused by lightning.

During a storm, the best thing a prepper can do is avoid being struck by lightning by any means necessary. They can begin by avoiding open areas, tall trees, and poles, as well as standing on insulating material to avoid being caught off guard.

## Having been poisoned

There is also a much greater risk of coming into contact with poisonous plants, which can cause physical discomfort. You should not only become acquainted with these plants but also make an effort to find the best remedy for them. As a responsible prepper, the best thing you can do is find inexpensive and convenient ways to avoid poisonous plants like poison ivy and poison oak.

The good news is that these plants are easy to identify and thus avoid. However, there are some instances where you may unknowingly come into contact with them. If this is the case, you'll need to know a thing or two about getting rid of the poison before the side effects kick in and cause you even more pain.

Prevention is always better than cure, so get into the habit of always wearing long sleeves, thick gloves, long pants, and a pair of gumboots. This type of clothing will protect you (and your group)

# PREPPER'S LONG-TERM SURVIVAL GUIDE

from coming into contact with these plants while out in the wild, whether for hunting or camping. The sooner you begin treatment for these ailments, the better.

### Tick-bone illness

The tick-borne disease should also be on your radar because it can make survival in the wilderness extremely difficult. Ticks prefer moist, hidden areas such as the groin, armpits, and scalp. Tick bites can also serve as an entry point for bacteria and bacterial infections and sucking your blood. The latter is why ticks must be identified and removed as soon as possible.

Removing ticks as soon as they are discovered and treating your clothing with tick-repellant chemicals will save you the trouble of entertaining these opportunistic parasites.

### Infection prevention

Hands should be disinfected with antibacterial hand wipes before touching any wounds. Before touching anything, apply sanitized gel or spray to your hands. Avoid using public restrooms if you don't want to spread bacteria and become infected.

For assistance in the primary care of wounds, a total body washing station comprising lancets, alcohol wipes, alcohol swabs, a thermometer for measuring body temperature, and a thermometer tape measure would be appropriate.

Clean wounds & disinfect foot ulcers with a portable foot bath. It's suitable for cleaning, but it doesn't have any antibacterial properties. Therefore, the harm will spread.

Any bandages or medical tape that the FDA has approved can be used. Please double-check that they are latex-free and safe to use on wounds or human skin. You may also want to buy a particular brand of medical tape because some include silicone, which can cause skin irritation or burning if you don't notice it immediately.

### Treating hyperthermia

Hyperthermia is also called heatstroke and is just as dangerous as hypothermia. Knowing the symptoms could save lives, including your own. Treatment may include increasing your fluid intake, resting in the shade, or placing a damp cloth on the back of your neck to lower your body temperature.

Heat exhaustion is a condition caused by prolonged exposure to high temperatures combined with a lack of water consumption. Headaches, nausea, vomiting, dizziness, muscle cramps, a weak pulse, profuse sweating, and chilly skin are all signs of heat exhaustion. Place the person in a shady area. If you can't move them, cover them with something to keep the sun out. Give them water in little doses and cover their heads with a cold towel. You may gradually lower their body temperature this way.

The first one is heated sickness and often occurs in boiling areas and can affect anyone. Some of the symptoms include dehydration and too much sweating as the body attempts to cool itself.

There might be heat exhaustion since the body goes into overdrive as it tries to cool and, at the same time, save water that has been rapidly lost. The people who are most affected by heat illness include the elderly, the very young, those with chronic ailments, and those who consume lots of alcohol.

As a prepper, you need to make sure that you are doing all in your power to get the desired people watched and be on high alert, especially when venturing into areas that are known for their heat.

# HEALTH

If a person suffers from heat illness, it would be a good idea to take them to a cool place, and give them chilled fluids (and not cold). Evaporative cooling will also go a long way in getting their body temperatures to drop drastically.

## Reactions to allergens

Allergic reactions happen when the immune system's response to a foreign substance is exaggerated. Anaphylaxis, a potentially fatal condition, may occur if the reaction is severe enough. If you see someone having an allergic reaction, inquire about their allergies. If they do, they might have a pi-pen, which you could use to help them feel better. Allow the individual to lie on their back with their feet elevated. They should remove their clothing to allow them to breathe more freely. No water, food, or medication should be given to them orally. Check to see if the person's clothes are loose and if they can breathe. If you used the pi-Pen, wait about 15 minutes. If the reaction persists, you should administer a second dose.

## Dehydration

Dehydration is another serious condition that can have serious consequences if not treated promptly. There are numerous ways to lose a large amount of water, including respiration, perspiration, and urination. Prolonged diarrhea is another common reason for people to lose a lot of water (as well as other vital nutrients).

A good survivalist will be on the lookout for symptoms such as nausea, muscle cramps, dizziness, and vomiting. Dehydration causes an imbalance in the organic electrolytes, which has a negative impact on them. Always exercise caution when rehydrating because excessive water intake during dehydration can result in water poisoning in your body due to excessive sodium loss, particularly during perspiration.

You are well-hydrated if your urine is light yellow to almost colorless. You should season your water with salt and drink slowly rather than all at once. You should also consider resting while replacing electrolytes so that the body can return to normal electrolyte balance.

Always treat dehydration with the seriousness it deserves because it is the only way to survive. It is critical to read the signs your body sends out, and if you suspect you are dehydrated, take the necessary steps to combat it.

Proper circulation is essential during rehydration because it allows the treated water to reach all parts of your body and restore ironic balance. Remember to remove extra clothing in hot weather because it will only cause more sweating and thus more water loss. In cold weather, keep clothing on but loosen it slightly to allow for proper circulation. Finally, remember to rest in order to speed up your return to normalcy.

## Fall

Remove any clothing that could restrict a person's movement if they have fallen and may have broken bones or other injuries. Then, as gently as possible, transfer them to a flat surface while applying pressure to any open wounds. If the person is awake and responsive, inquire about any neck or back pain. If this is the case, gently press both sides of these areas and have them wiggle their toes to check for numbness. Finally, if there is any swelling or discoloration around the joints, test it by gently shifting the joint.

### Taking care of burns

Minor burns just need the application of cold (but not ice) water to the affected area, followed by the use of an ointment to keep it moist. Keep the blisters intact and the injury away from direct sunlight. To avoid infection, don't put anything on the wound; instead, cover it with a loose cloth. If the injured person is in a lot of pain, give them medication to help them feel better.

If there are any chemicals on the burn, thoroughly rinse the area with water until it stops burning. After that, cover the burn with a clean bandage to prevent infection. Apply no creams or lotions to the burned area for at least 24 hours, and avoid lifting anything heavy on top of it.

Burns can happen even if you are careful. They can be caused by a campfire, touching a hot surface like a kettle, or spilling boiling water on yourself. You may lose several layers of your skin, depending on the severity, leaving you vulnerable to infection which could kill you in a survival situation. You should know how to treat minor, as well as 2nd and 3rd degree burns with first aid supplies. It can be tricky as you need to protect the wound whilst still allowing the wound to breathe and monitoring it carefully.

Again, it cannot be stressed enough how important and advantageous it is to take a credible first aid course, not only for survival situations in the wilderness but also for everyday life.

### Diabetes-related shock

If you suspect someone has diabetic shock, take them to the hospital right away. Then, examine their airway, breathing patterns, and mental state. Take their blood sugar levels every few minutes if possible to see if they improve and to keep them as hydrated as possible.

### Caring for wounds

Even the smallest cuts will require frequent bandage changes, so bandages will definitely be one of those things that you'll want to add to your medical kit, preferably as many as you can. You can avoid stockpiling large amounts of bandages if you learn how to make your own. You can make them out of clean clothes, such as t-shirts, by cutting out rectangles or squares of material, but remember to wash them properly before you use them as dressings for wounds. Butterfly stitches are an item that you really need to add to your kit as they are needed when you have to close an open wound and are quite hard to improvise. You need to disinfect every single wound; ideally, you would be using antibiotic ointment, but petroleum jelly is quite efficient if that is not available. Rubbing alcohol is also great for cleaning wounds, the aim here is to keep the wound as clean as you possibly can to avoid infections.

### Frostbite

Another common survival ailment is none other than frostbite, and this happens when both the skin as well as the underlying tissues are frozen. The extent of frostbite can be rated from first to third degree, and a prepper needs to know how to act to prevent getting to the point where they have third-degree frostbites because this might call for amputation.

The first—and second—degree frostbites always heal in time, but third-degree frostbites are permanent since both the skin and the underlying tissues freeze permanently. It is, therefore, necessary to prevent frostbites from happening by getting the right kind of attire before heading out into the cold or freezing areas.

# HEALTH

Once you feel as though you are starting to freeze too much, it is important to get to warm water and take a bath. It might be uncomfortable for a moment, but in the end, your body will pick up the heat, and you will be okay in a short moment. Never tamper with any blisters that might have formed in the process but if the skin is broken, then keep it clean just like any other wound right before dressing it with clean bandages.

## Snakebite

It is common to encounter snakes in the wild, and so an accomplished survivalist; one needs to know a thing or two about combating snakebite and its devastating effects. Some snakes have more lethal venom than others, but either way, they should all be treated with the same kind of urgency as they can all result in bad health.

You should also take care of nonvenomous snakebites because their sharp teeth puncture the skin (which is a protective barrier). Punctured skin in the wild can be the perfect entry point for harmful bacteria, viruses or microorganisms, and parasites. Always be on the lookout for coral snakes and pit vipers because these two are known for their very dangerous venom.

Preppers are always urged to watch their every step and where they perch on trees because snakes are most likely to be found. Examples of pit vipers include de lances, water moccasins, rattlesnakes, and copperheads. Coral snakes are related to cobras, and if you know anything about cobras, then you know how precise and deadly their strikes can be.

For that matter, having the proper medical kit ready to combat any form of time painful snakebite should come in handy for you. You can also cleanse the bitten area with clean water to elevate any possibility of being infected. Do not attempt cutting the bite marks and sucking the venom out like it is done in the movies because doing so will only make matters worse for you.

## Survival Medicine Guide

Keep a list of drugs, dosage, and usage. The unexpected events are stressful, so one shouldn't depend on recollection to substitute drugs. What if one's debilitated and requires a long-term pill? Will SAR know oner medication?

## Understand the medication supply

To keep track of medicine expiration dates, use an almanac or an app. This allows for refills and serves as an emergency reference. If an emergency threatens oner pharmacy, a person would be able to monitor how much medication is left and if early refills are required.

## Place pills in tightly sealed containers

Medicines can be stored in hospital cabinets or in a plastic pill container. If a community is at risk of flooding or heavy rain, store oner medicines in a watertight jar. If medications have come into contact with flood water, only use them if absolutely necessary.

## Place drugs in a cooler to keep them cool

Earthquakes, forest fires, and storms have the potential to disrupt the grid. What would you do if your refrigerator broke down? Anyone who uses refrigerated drugs should carry a small cooler, preferably a less-messy gel cooler. Inquire with your pharmacist or doctor whether your medications need to be refrigerated.

# PREPPER'S LONG-TERM SURVIVAL GUIDE

When a patient requires critical medications right away, any pharmacy can provide them. Examples include inhalants, insulin, and antibiotics. Consider the following constraints when incorporating emergency fills into your overall emergency plan:

- Prescriptions are required for emergency fills.
- A seven-day emergency supply is the maximum.
- Before requesting reimbursement, prescriptions must be paid in full at the pharmacy. The reimbursement amount is determined by the plan.
- Many health insurers do not reimburse due to pharmacy jurisdiction.
- The emergency fill regulations are determined by the Oner health insurance plan (including which prescriptions are approved).
- For non-emergency refills, contact the oner doctor.

Different people have various requirements. For three days of survival in Vermont, consistent heat and heavy blankets may be required. In Hawaii, one extra blanket may suffice. Consider the type of emergency the person might face. The CDC recommends purchasing earthquake-resistant goods. In flood-prone areas, keep supplies dry in case of an escape in water.

## Car and office bags

One cannot keep as many supplies for survival in one automobile or at work as one can at home. Emergencies can occur at any time, so plan ahead of time.

## Using an Emergency Plan Template

The DHS and Red Cross both provide emergency plan templates. A guide may also be available from local or state governments. This one for Montgomery County, Maryland, includes utility company numbers and radio station frequencies.

## Early preparation reduces confusion

In chaotic situations, good emergency planning provides certainty. It will be decided how to obtain the next insulin dosage. Preparing now may protect the health of the Oner family.

## Pain relievers and fever reducers

These are most likely the first medications you will use. Although pains and fevers are defensive mechanisms used by your body to alert you to a situation or, in the case of fever, to try to fight an infection, no one enjoys feeling these things. Whether you stock up on aspirin, ibuprofen, or acetaminophen, one thing you must know is the correct dosage. To increase your stockpile, take these only if you have severe aches or prolonged fever, for example.

Here's a quick list of medications to keep in your medicine cabinet: Cold remedies, such as NyQuil cough syrup; pain relievers, such as ibuprofen, paracetamol, or aspirin stomach pains Imodium and other antacids a month's supply of prescription medication

## Aches in the stomach

This could be a problem, especially if you've drastically altered your diet. Anxiety and other types of stress can also cause stomach pain. Imodium, for example, is an excellent treatment for this. You might prefer tablets over liquids in this case because you can stockpile more of them. Antacids can help with heartburn and nausea, but everyone is different, so figure out which one works best for you.

# HEALTH

## Medications on prescription

Depending on your condition, not having access to your prescription medications can have varying degrees of severity. Untreated psychiatric or cardiovascular issues, for example, can be extremely dangerous. The main issue is that you may not be able to stockpile this type of medication because doctors frequently prescribe it in small amounts. You should consult your doctor and inform them that you are preparing for an emergency. Make sure you have enough stock to last a month or two. You might want to learn what happens if you suddenly stop taking your prescribed medication and what you can do to mitigate the effects of withdrawal.

## Insulin

Diabetes is becoming more common. This could be due to our overall diet and lack of exercise. Whatever the reason, if you or a member of your family requires insulin and is unable to obtain it, you must consider how this may affect you or a family member. The first thing you should try to figure out is how to control the disease without using it. A controlled diet should be used to accomplish this, though this is not a long-term solution. Some insulin medications can be stored for up to a year in certain conditions, so switching to those types of insulin must be a step you must take and discuss with your doctor. However, depending on the disaster, it may be difficult to store the insulin correctly.

## Birth Restrictions

With so much going on in a disaster, procreation can be a means of escape, and it is undoubtedly a compulsion shared by all species on the planet. It can also be used to relieve stress. The longer the emergency situation lasts, the more likely this will occur. So stockpiling birth control pills could be a good way to avoid giving birth in an emergency. It is important to remember that giving birth without proper medical care can be dangerous for both the mother and the child, so do everything you can to avoid this until the situation normalizes.

Besides, even if both the mother and the baby survive the birth, without proper medical care, most kids might not live more than a year. Even though many women give birth without medical attention, this is not something that you should plan to do, given the situation. Also, if you don't have a regular partner, you might want to stockpile condoms too, as sexually transmitted diseases, without proper medical care, can turn into a risky situation.

## Keeping Your First-Aid Kit Current

Examine your first-aid kit twice a year to ensure that everything is up-to-date and in good working order. You may also use this opportunity to sanitize the bag in which you keep your equipment and any non-packaged utensils. Remove everything from the bag and spray it with antiseptic. Spray the tweezers, scissors, and anything else that can resist moisture while you wait for the bag to dry. Then go through the rest of your belongings to see if there's anything you need to get rid of or replace. Another reason for labeling items is to keep track of them. You may also make a checklist with labels to ensure that you don't forget to restock any essential items in your kit. Examine the seals of individual packages, especially if the item contains adhesives or medicines. If any of them seem suspicious (have holes or moisture), they should not be used on or near an open wound. You should get rid of them and replace them with new ones.

If you keep your items in a watertight, puncture-resistant, and drop-resistant bag, and make sure your kit can't be tampered with, most of your items should last for years. Gauzes, bandages, and metal utensils have an almost limitless lifespan. Even the ones that aren't generally used for a long time beyond their expiration date. The same may be said for most over-the-counter medications. Most drugs have an expiration date that is anywhere from 12 to 60 months after they were made, but that doesn't mean they can't be used after that.

The expiration date, on the other hand, considers storage and handling. For example, if a pharmacist removes a medication from its original package and places it in another container, the drug's potency, lifespan, and safety may be affected. It is recommended that the medication in your first aid kit be kept in a sealed manufacturer's container for stress-free handling.

Most over-the-counter medications in tablet or capsule form retain their potency for 3-5 years beyond their expiration date if kept in an unopened container. Liquid medications are a different story since they include extra ingredients that might become unstable beyond the expiration date. In fact, you should check any liquids in your pack first, whether they're medications, disinfectants, or anything else. It's time to replace them if they're foggy, discolored, have become too thick or liquid, or smell awful.

Pi-Pens and antibiotics are the two most important exceptions to the use beyond the expiration date rule. Pi-Pens contain a substance called epinephrine, which swiftly degrades beyond its expiration date. Similarly, most antibiotics will degrade quickly beyond their expiration date, even if they are unopened and stored in a cold, dark, and dry environment. Antibiotics may only be used for a few weeks or months, regardless of their stated expiration date. Antibiotics, whether in tablet or capsule form, should be kept in your first-aid kit unopened. Spray antibiotics may be used, but they must be replaced six months after being used. They wouldn't be safe to use on an open wound otherwise.

In terms of specific dates, here are some guidelines for how long you should keep medications in your first aid kit:

- It can be used for up to 5 years after opening, regardless of the expiration date. It has been dormant for more than a decade.
- Tylenol should be used within 5 years of opening. The same holds true for its unopened form, as it loses potency after 5 years.
- Aspirin is most effective when taken within 4-5 years of surgery. Its pain-relieving properties may fade significantly after that, but its blood-thinning properties will deteriorate much faster.
- Antibiotics: Most antibiotics can be stored for up to a year if not used. Prescription antibiotics should be taken as soon as possible, and generic antibiotics (primarily topical) should be taken within 6-12 months.
- Cough Syrup: Use within 24-36 months of the expiration date if unopened. When you open it, the liquid is contaminated and begins to degrade, so use it within a few weeks.
- Nasal Sprays: Nasal decongestants degrade quickly because they contain preservatives. It's best to use them within a few weeks of opening, or at the very least before they expire.
- Prescription Medication: Because of the medication's potency, manufacturers limit its use to one year after prescription. They usually have an expiration date of less than a year after they were prescribed, after which they are no longer safe to use.

## CHAPTER 2: NATURAL REMEDIES

### Know Your Herb

Mother Nature can be tricky when it comes to identifying her bounty. For example, Rose-bay Willow is a clone of Purple Loose-strife, which is used to treat diarrhea caused by typhoid fever or dysentery. The two plants look exactly like rookie Rose rustlers (my term for plant hunters). This could be dangerous because each plant has its own set of properties. Bring a field guide with you if you're unsure so you can quickly identify what you're looking at.

Lead levels are one of them, for obvious reasons. You should also keep a low profile and avoid areas that are open to the public.

There are many reasons to start learning how to identify medicinal and edible plants, but the most important reason is to start NOW. You'll realize that once you start, you'll never be able to stop.

Mother Nature's pharmacy contains hundreds of plants and herbs that people can use to heal themselves. Your list of home remedies is about to become a lot more interesting. Despite these natural herbs being used for hundreds of years, doctors and scientists are now recommending their use for healing. Traditional healing methods can easily replace these natural medical resources. To name a few, the plants have the ability to heal and reduce cholesterol, high blood pressure, and arthritis pain. Some of the best healing herbs can also be used to treat cancer cells and even help alcoholics quit drinking.

Herbs, other natural remedies, and natural medical resources are all as effective as conventional treatments. They can be even more effective and have no negative side effects. Here are some of the most effective natural medical resources. These super healers can be added to your natural medicine or herbal products cabinet, along with your favorite recipes. If you incorporate some of them into your daily routine, they can be beneficial to your body.

## Aloe Vera Gel

Aloe vera has traditionally been used to treat skin conditions, constipation, infections, worm infestations, and colic. In Chinese medicine, it is widely used to treat a variety of fungal diseases. In modern times, the herb is used to soften the skin in a variety of cosmetic products. Surprisingly, there are over 78 active ingredients in Aloe Vera. Furthermore, studies have shown that the herb has antiviral, anti-inflammatory, and antifungal properties. It boosts the immune system and contains no known allergens.

Everyone should have this plant because of its miraculous healing properties. Simply break off one of its fleshy leaves and apply the gel inside to relieve pain and provide a soothing sensation. A mild laxative can be obtained by extracting the gel from a large leaf and placing it in a glass of water.

## Dandelion

Not only is dandelion delicious, its leaves are full of beta-carotene and vitamin C, this fantastic herb also has bile stimulating properties which in turn improves the body's ability to get rid of toxins. This is helpful if you have trouble finding fresh, running water and your body is constantly bombarded with bacteria.

## Lemon balm

I highly recommend growing this aromatic plant. I've been happy with this plant this year which has produced an abundance of fragrant, lemony leaves; when used as a tea, it can calm and soothe agitation and irritability. It can be used just before bed because it has a calming effect. Lemon balm is also good for stomach upset. It's not good for pregnant women, though, because it stimulates the uterus.

# PREPPER'S LONG-TERM SURVIVAL GUIDE

### New England Aster

This lovely aromatic flower can be found almost anywhere, but it thrives in places like abandoned lots and fields. It has a wide range of amazing applications, particularly for those suffering from asthma or COPD (Chronic obstructive pulmonary disease). New England Aster is used primarily as an expectorant, relieving cold-induced coughs and expelling phlegm. Eating its fresh flowers produces a relaxing, drowsy feeling.

### Blood Flower

Here's a useful plant for those of you who eat poisonous berries or other plants you're not sure about. Related to milkweed, its milky sap can be used as an emetic. (It makes you vomit). In addition, the sap can be used to relieve the pain of nettle and insect bites.

### Catnip

In addition to driving your cat crazy, medically, I think it will drive you crazy. It, like NyQuil, relieves cold symptoms, can stop bleeding and swelling, and acts as an icebreaker because it promotes sweating. This plant, which is a member of the mint family, can help with gastrointestinal issues, menstrual cramps, and migraines.

### Sage

Sage is my final pick for "must-know" plants. When most people think of sage, they think of Thanksgiving stuffing. However, when it comes to super healing plants, this is my top pick. Sage has antifungal, anti-inflammatory, and antioxidant properties. Sage was used to preserving meat before the invention of the refrigerator, which is ideal if you're on a meat hunt. Sage is effective against colds, aids digestion, combats diarrhea, reduces inflammation and swelling, dries phlegm, relieves cramps, can be used as an ointment for cuts and bruises, kills bacteria, and is even said to restore color to gray hair.

### Turmeric

Turmeric contains antioxidant, anti-inflammatory and anti-cancer properties. Who ever thought that an ingredient used for flavor in curries can help relieve pain? This spice that is popular for its use in curries contains curcumin which helps treat arthritis. Curcumin is a potent anti-inflammatory and an essential component that works similarly to Cox-2 inhibitor drugs in reducing the Cox-2 enzyme that causes arthritis swelling.

### Cinnamon

A recent study on type-2 diabetics showed that daily intake of cinnamon extract reduces the body's blood sugar level by 10%. It reduces heart-related risks and lowers cholesterol by about 13%. 1 g of cinnamon extract capsules every day helps tame blood sugar, while 1 to 6 g capsules reduce cholesterol. However, a large amount of the current spice is not good for your health. Therefore, it is better to stick to the water-soluble extract.

### Rosemary

Heterocyclic amines, or HCAs, are important carcinogens found in a variety of cancers. These amines are produced when meat is grilled, fried, or roasted at high temperatures. HCA levels in the body are reduced by rosemary extract, which is a common powder mixed into meat after cooking.

# HEALTH

Carcinogens are also prevented from binding to DNA and entering the body by rosemary extract. It is the first step in the development of cancer, and rosemary extracts can help prevent cancer at this stage. As a result, taking rosemary extract kills carcinogens before they become tumors. Although this study was limited to animals, the extract appears to have anti-cancer properties. Add rosemary extract to any spice blend to help reduce HCAs in the body. It will also enhance the flavor of the dish, making it more flavorful. For a perfect blend, combine the herb with oregano, parsley, thyme, and onions.

## Ginger

Motion sickness, pregnancy, and chemotherapy are just a few of the things that ginger can help with. This is an old home remedy that our mothers and grandmothers often tell us about. They are correct because it does work! Ginger is a potent antioxidant that inhibits serotonin's effects in the body. When you feel nauseous, your stomach and body produce this chemical, which inhibits the production of free radicals, which is another cause of stomach pain.

## Garlic

High consumption of garlic has cured colorectal and ovarian cancer. People have also experienced a reduction in the number and size of precancerous growths. Garlic's benefits are not limited to cancer prevention; it also helps lower blood pressure. Garlic contains approximately 70 active phytochemicals, including allicin, which has been shown to reduce blood pressure by 30 points. Garlic in your diet slows arterial blockages and prevents strokes. Fresh, crushed garlic offers the best cancer and cardiovascular benefits. However, one should have at least five cloves of crushed garlic to enjoy the maximum benefits.

## Holy Basil

Several animal studies support holy basil, a special variety of the plant that is used in pesto, holy basil is effective in reducing stress by increasing norepinephrine and adrenaline and decreasing serotonin in the body. The herb is also popular for relieving headaches and indigestion. Holy basil tea leaves are a great natural resource that is more effective than traditional methods of pain relief.

## Feverfew

This well-known herb has been used for centuries to relieve headaches, toothaches, stomachaches, infertility, menstrual problems and labor during childbirth. The healing effect comes from a biochemical in the herb known as parthenolide. It fights the widening of blood vessels during migraines. The herb also prevents blood clots, dizziness, relieves allergies and reduces the pain of arthritis.

## St. John's Wort

St. John's wort is not only used to treat physical symptoms but also to relieve mild to moderate anxiety and depression. Best of all, it works as effectively as any other medication without any side effects.

## Saw Palmetto

Saw palmetto is a supplement that men take in order to treat prostate cancer. Additionally, it contributes to a number of men's health problems, including hair loss, low libido, and prostate enlargement. Apart from that, it is said to aid in relaxation, treat respiratory conditions, and strengthen the immune system.

## How to Create a Home Medicine Cabinet Using Natural Remedies

Here is a list of medicines for probable problems while surviving a catastrophic event. All the medicines are naturally occurring, so one may start preparing an organic medicine cabinet in case there is a prediction of a disaster.

### Respiratory

- **Elderberry syrup:** This is useful for respiratory issues as well as for boosting your immune system all year. Although Lexie's Homemade kit has recently gained popularity, this is still the brand preference among Amazon customers. Yum V's Immunity Shield candies are preferred by children. You will appreciate that they are sweetened with glucose rather than sugar, but be cautious if you have a dog, as glucose is extremely toxic to dogs.
- **Essential oil of eucalyptus:** It must be diluted with canola oil and applied to the chest or pajamas so that people can smell it all night. When combined with bath salts, you can also use it in your vaporizer for volatile oils or baths. Remember that children should not be exposed to eucalyptus oil.
- **Humidifier with a cool spray:** Although not strictly medicines, people use them in their beds to facilitate clean breathing.
- **Trilight Health's Lympha Rub:** If you don't want to make your own lavender oil and plants, this is a great massage for inflamed lymph nodes.
- **Essential oil diffuser:** This is not the same as a humidifier. It is beneficial to diffuse respiratory-supportive oils into the air. There are numerous diffusers available on various platforms; however, we personally have many of this specific type that we use in various areas of our house.
- **Plant-based respiratory blends:** These volatile oil blends are both efficient and cost-effective.

### Ear Medications

- **Garlic oil drops:** Rotate garlic and liquid silver.
- **Colloidal silver:** A few drops of it in your lobes will undoubtedly help. It almost looks like a natural antimicrobial alternative!
- **Trilight Healthy Person's Ear Infection Relief Kit:** This is an excellent kit to have on hand.

### Providing First Aid

- **Lavender essential oil** is great for scrapes, wounds, and burns.
- **Bentonite clay:** This is a must-have! People like the Redmond Sand brand.
- **Essential oil of Frankincense:** This can be used to remove an abscess hair lump. Furthermore, it is effective almost everywhere that needs to be repaired.
- **Make your own antibacterial hand soap:** (or one can buy some non-toxic soap refills here).
- **Make your own coconut oil stick**: People frequently use plain coconut oil to soothe cuts and other wounds.
- **Arnica pellets** for pain relief
- **Eczema Cream** by Earth Mama Organics
- **Rocky Mountain Oils' Ouchie**

### Stomach Medicines

- **Peppermint essential oil:** applied to the stomach after diluting with canola oil • Activated charcoal
- **Probiotics:** These are also excellent for general health!
- **Ginger tea:** Ginger is excellent for nausea relief.

### Cough/Cold/Flu medications

- **Vitamin C:** People consume more vitamin C when they are sick, but they also consume it on a regular basis throughout the winter.
- **Neti pot:** This will be great for cleaning out my nasal passageways! It is critical to use clean water for

# HEALTH

this. Our water is frequently heated before being allowed to cool.
- **Vitamin D3:** Vitamin D3 is essential for immune system health! People take it on a regular basis throughout the winter, similar to Vitamin C, but if one of us is ill, I make sure everyone gets enough Vitamin D3.
- **Oscillococcinum:** The use of these homeopathic pellets may alleviate flu-like symptoms.
- **Cold Calm:** These homeopathic pills dissolve in the mouth, reducing symptoms significantly!

## Medications for Pain
- Lemon water for the throat
- Tea for Throat Coat
- Cinnamon with local, raw honey

## Pain and ache medications
- Arnica lotion
- To detoxify your bath, use bath salts or volcanic clay.

## Seasonal Allergy Medicines
- Raw, local honey pot saline solution
- Lavender essential oil
- Lemon essential oil
- Eucalyptus essential oil

# BOOK 9: BUG OUT

## BUG OUT
# WHEN YOUR HOME IS NO LONGER SAFE

When a calamity strikes and your present location is unsafe, bugging out implies fleeing the region. Anyone bugging out should expect to leave their house and possessions behind, with no prospect of ever seeing them again.

In reality, bugging out might be a result of a short-term tragedy, but it can be a long-term solution. In most cases, you should depart for a specific bug-out spot. Ideally, you've previously considered and planned your bug out site in the event of a calamity. This should be a secure spot away from crowded areas, providing you with sufficient natural resources and a feeling of security.

The Bug Out Bag (B.O.B.), also known as the Go-To Bag, is a survival pack meant to keep you alive for a minimum of 3 days. The purpose of a bug-out bag is not for long-term survival but rather as an emergency bag when you need to evacuate quickly.

Whether it's an imminent natural disaster, a chemical spill, or a terrorist attack that threatens your home, you should be able to grab your bug-out bag and get out fast to safer ground. While in most scenarios bugging in at your home is a safer plan than bugging out to places unknown, part of prepping is being prepared for every possibility. For that reason, you should begin your life as a prepper by putting together a bug-out bag to prepare for a home evacuation if need be.

**When should one Decide to Bug Out?**

The most obvious reasons to bug out are if the location of your home will be the point of impact for the calamity or catastrophic event or if you are caught away from your home when the emergency strikes. These are two important and specific reasons for you to bug out and seek survival! Other unusual reasons why you might want to bug out of your house include:

- If your home is not physically safe, such as the aftermath of a natural disaster, floodwaters in your home, or a burned-out house.
- Staying away from the house for a while can make you feel better if someone is specifically targeting you or threatening you.
- If you run out of supplies and are unable to locate any more in your area.
- If there is a civil unrest situation around the corner and the mobs become violent.
- If the government specifies that your house, neighborhood, and block will not receive any assistance and that you must vacate the area.

Perfect situational awareness is required to determine when to bug out and when to bug in. A prepper's job is to be aware of everything that is going on around him/her and the family. It is the only way to determine whether to gather supplies for bugging in or pack a bag for bugging out.

**Bug-Out Checklist**

- **Electronic Items:** Assorted batteries, 2–3 flashlights, GPS, Radio (solar), Radio (CB).
- **First Aid:** Antibiotics, Aspirin, Bandages (assorted sizes), Bandana, Cloth, Cough Drops, Gauze Pads, Gloves (plastic), Ibuprofen, Mirror, Needles and Thread, Tape, Space Blanket, Tweezers, Tylenol.
- **Fire and Shelter:** Bandana, Candles, Charred Cloth, Clothes (coat, gator, gloves, hat, jacket, pants, socks), Cord, Cotton Balls, Glow Sticks (avoid red), Magnesium Flint Striker, Matches, Poncho, Rope, Sleeping Bag, 1–2 Space Blankets, Tarp, Tent (optional), Wool Blanket.
- **Food and Water:** Bottled Water (2–4 bottles), Canteen, Fishing Equipment, Water Filter, MREs, Protein Bars, Water Purification Tablets, Salt, Spices, Sugar.
- **Hygiene:** Chap Stick, Comb, Hand Sanitizer, Mirror (compact), Toilet Paper/Tissues, Toothbrush, Toothpaste, Soap Bars, Sunscreen.

- **Weapons and Tools:** 3 Knives (Swiss Army-style, folding knife, fixed-blade belt knife), Duct Tape, Handsaw, Hatchet, Machete, Multi-Tool, Shovel (folding).

## How to Make a Bug-Out Bag?

***Capacity and volume.*** The first thing to look for in a bug-out bag is the volume and capacity of the backpack. However, many preppers are perplexed because, while some backpacks claim to hold the same capacity, not all of those backpacks can hold the same amount of gear due to the arrangement and design of their compartments.

Look for backpacks with multiple large and small compartments that can all be easily sealed with a zipper, Velcro, sealed pockets, etc. This will ensure that your backpack can hold as much gear as possible while traveling without losing any of it.

Look for a backpack with a volume of 40 liters/2,500 cubic inches if you want to get through the day. Look for a backpack with a capacity of 50 to 60 liters/4,000 cubic inches to last three days, which is what most bug-out bags are designed to do. Increase the capacity to 6,000 cubic inches/80 to 90 liters for a backpack designed to last a week. If you're looking for a backpack that can hold enough gear to keep you going for more than a week, you're probably not considering what your body can physically handle.

***Frame.*** After deciding on the capacity of your bug-out bag, you must decide on the type of frame your bug-out bag will be mounted on. There are two types of backpack frames: internal frames and external frames. An aluminum frame will be located inside the backpack of internal frame packs. They are far more adaptable than external frame backpacks because they shift the weight of the pack from the shoulders to the hips.

Furthermore, internal frame backpacks are slightly lighter and smaller than external frame backpacks, so if you need a pack with 90 liters of capacity to hold enough gear and supplies to last you a week, an internal frame setup is probably not the best option for you. However, the vast majority of bug-out bags are only designed to last three days, so an internal frame backpack should be seriously considered in that regard.

External frame backpacks are larger, stronger, and heavier than internal frame backpacks. Rather than having an aluminum frame placed inside the pack, as the name implies, the frame supports the backpack from the outside. The ability to attach more gear and supplies to an external frame backpack is a benefit. External frame backpacks are commonly used by backpackers to attach heavy-duty items such as sleeping bags, tents, coats, and so on.

Overall, if you want a pack that will last you a week or more, the external frame backpack is the way to go. Choose the internal frame for a more traditional three-day bug-out bag due to its lighter weight.

***Build with care.*** After you've decided on the capacity and frame of your backpack, the next thing to consider is the build quality. Your backpack should be built to withstand harsh conditions and be water-resistant, the zippers should function smoothly, and the straps should be thick and adjustable. When purchasing a backpack in person, you should be able to tell if the material is tough and durable simply by feeling and handling it.

If you're looking for a good deal on eBay or Amazon, it'll be a little more difficult to tell if the pack is durable, but online reviews and item descriptions should provide you with all the information you need. Furthermore, if you receive the backpack in the mail and it appears to be poorly constructed, you can always return it. Military-grade packs, such as an Alice Pack or Three-Day Deployment Bags, are the best backpacks to look for.

***Color.*** Last but not least, you must choose a color. Contrary to popular belief, you should avoid more camouflage or tactical type colors because they identify you as a law enforcement or military person. When the grid is down, you want to blend in rather than stand out. As a result, look for more neutral colors. Green, brown, grey, or even dark blue should work well because they allow you to hide if necessary while also making you stand out when seen. Avoid using bright colors such as red, orange, yellow, or pink.

Survival equipment with this knowledge, you will be able to select the best bug-out bag for you. The next step is the most enjoyable: filling it up! As a hint, you should buy all of your gear BEFORE purchasing your bug-out bag so that you know the general size and type of backpack you require. When you've packed your bug-out bag, make sure it's well-organized, with the most important items in easy-to-reach places.

Irrespective of whether you are about to experience natural disasters at your residing location or the area is about to experience serious riots. You will have to head out to a different shelter or location. This is termed bugging out! You need to decide upon the composition choice for objects included within the backpack in such situations. It will completely depend upon the first distinction! The next consideration is deciding where you would be moving to deal with the emergency. It will be the bug-out location for you!

After you have decided upon these two things, there are other considerations upon the paths you must take, the measures you will use, the difficulties you might encounter, and other such aspects. Before you learn how to prepare your bug-out bag, answering all of these consideration factors is important. Remember, when you bug in, you have the potential to stock up supplies for two weeks or more, but you cannot expect to do the same when you are bugging out. It is because you will be limited on the bags and things that you can carry! Therefore, you might have to follow the 72-hour rule here, as it is the specified time for the bugging-out preppers until they get aid from hired authorities.

The things you will need within the bug-out bag or BOB are specified with just three elements; food, shelter, and clothing. The process of setting up the BOB is as follows:

You should get a lightweight and compact backpack, which should be a maximum of 30 liters. Do not go for a big bulky bag with the mindset of storing almost everything in your house. It will make you feel like you are in military training and will strain your body while carrying it a long distance. Make sure you get a good quality bag, as it will be holding your valuables, essentials, and survival goods. You don't want the bag to compromise in any manner to get you in trouble of surviving the crisis.

The bag should consist of groceries, a small stove, some cutlery, small cookware, and others. This will allow you to make hot food or drink, which will keep you active and healthy to deal with tough circumstances.

Choose foods that require less water to cook because you will not be at home with gallons of water to spare for cooking. You're on the move! And water is required for much more than just food production. An adult's daily water requirement is approximately 2 liters. You can't bring 6 liters of water in your bag; you can count on at least 3! Every member of your family should have their own

# PREPPER'S LONG-TERM SURVIVAL GUIDE

BOB with a capacity of 3 liters. To reduce the weight on your shoulders, purify the water ahead of time or fill the bottles with purified water before leaving the house.

When the human body is under stress, it requires a great deal of care and attention. As a result, it is preferable to have some casual dresses in the bag, such as T-shirts, casual trousers, pants, and so on. Carry winter clothing if you are in a cold location or during the winter months. It is preferable to prepare a separate bag for each member of your family. This way, you'll have enough room to accommodate everyone's needs in their individual bags. If you have children, choose a bag that is even smaller.

Portable tents, tarps, base camps, and other shelter solutions should be kept in your bag. If you and your family leave in your car, it can serve as a safe haven. Carry some sleeping bags or isothermal blankets with you as an alternative.

A torch, Swiss knife, cash, first-aid kit, nylon cord, and backup mobile phone are some other items that can come in handy during an emergency. Depending on your needs, you can prioritize these items and pack all of them or just a few of them.

So, this is the best way to pack your BOB! The most important thing is to keep the bags in inaccessible areas. Remember that you are not going camping but rather fighting a survival battle. If you had to bug out of your house, the situation would be disastrous. So, don't just pack the essentials for camping; consider the survival factors, decide what you might need to be safe in various scenarios, and return home soon.

You should only pack or bring the necessities and leave out anything that may not be useful to you. Remember, if you go to the supermarket and buy everything you see, you will eventually become an accumulator and intend to take everything in the BOB that you purchased. But this is the incorrect approach! If you are forced to evacuate your home, do not bring anything that appears unwanted or that you will not use during your survival journey.

Some residents near the disaster site will deny leaving their homes or being evacuated. They have a special attachment to their homes and can't bear the thought of them being destroyed. Some people believe that something or someone will save them from the disaster, and they refuse to leave or be evacuated. As a result, you can conclude that they are poor planners. They must learn more about optimal prepping and be prepared for any situation or move that may arise. If you do not respond while there is still time, you may not have the opportunity to repent later.

As a result, if there is a Category 5 Hurricane warning in the area where your property is located, you will have no choice but to evacuate. If you have homeowner's insurance, you will be compensated to rebuild your home or property. But there is no resurrection for a lost life! When it comes to surviving natural disasters or catastrophic events, time is of the essence. If you are a prepper, you understand how critical it is to bug out in critical situations. Most disasters can be handled properly by taking shelter at home or bugging in. However, if your home is in the danger zone, you must immediately evacuate!

As a result, follow all of the steps outlined above to prepare your BOB and be prepared to bug out in extreme conditions.

In most cases, you should travel to a pre-planned bug-out location before anything happens. If you haven't already, you should think about and possibly plan a bug-out location for use in the event of a natural disaster. This should take place in a safe location away from densely populated areas of the city. It should give you a lot of natural resources as well as a sense of security.

Everyone's bug-out bag (BOB) will be different, but there are a few items that everyone should have on hand in case of a bug-out emergency.

***Food and water are critical.*** Don't forget to add condiments and spices to your dish. You may be hungry, but that doesn't mean your diet should be limited to 'edible' foods.

The first-aid package with ointments, bandages, and a suture kit is also included. Never forget that you'll need to know how to utilize the items in your first aid kit if you want it to be effective. See the whole first aid skills handbook for more information.

Items for personal hygiene and sanitation. This will assist you in maintaining a clean, pleasant, and healthy environment.

A flashlight, batteries, and fire-starting materials are all recommended. All of these things are very necessary for survival while you're on the go.

## How to Find a New Shelter

Having a shelter massively increases your chances of survival in harmful conditions. For example, suppose you are caught in a heavy rainstorm. You could quickly develop hypothermia even if the air temperature is not extremely cold because having wet clothes lowers your body temperature quickly. If you can't get under shelter and get dry, you may be in danger. The biggest threat you will face while out in the wild is loss of body heat, particularly at night when temperatures drop, and you are more likely to be inactive. A shelter is vital for reducing the loss of body heat.

A shelter also makes it possible to safely gather food and store your possessions. Some shelters could offer protection from animals or at least make it more difficult for animals to steal food. A shelter provides you with a spot to sleep at night and to carry resources to, and it may also make you more visible to rescue efforts. You can stack firewood inside to keep it dry or give damp wood a chance to dry out, and you will have far more ability to stay warm throughout the night.

For many people surviving in the wild, a shelter represents the ability to exert some control over the surrounding environment. It provides warmth, dryness, security, protection from the wind, and more. Don't underestimate the importance of a shelter, and prioritize learning how to build one if you spend any significant amount of time outdoors in remote places.

Among the most important skills to master in a survival situation, building a shelter is an absolute must. Not only will it protect you from the elements and predators, but it will also provide you with comfort and warmth. In addition to physical comfort, building a shelter is also beneficial for your mental and emotional state. To begin building your own shelter, you will need quality cordage and other building materials such as wood and an axe.

To begin building your own survival shelter, you will need to gather the necessary materials and find a suitable location. You will also need to assess your needs and design the structure. It is important to select a flat and dry site to avoid rainwater from entering your shelter. Finally, you will need to protect your shelter by covering it in some way. A simple tent is an excellent choice if you're in a hot climate, but don't forget about protection.

When building your shelter, keep in mind that it should be large enough for you and your family, but also small enough for your group. A large shelter will take up a lot of space, and it will be hard to keep warm inside it. A smaller shelter will be easier to conceal in. Remember that body heat is the fastest way to die in a survival situation. Many people die each year due to hypothermia.

After you have chosen a location, you'll need to evaluate the site. Choose a natural location, one that's naturally protected from wind and flooding. You should also consider building a rectangular frame from logs and filling it with debris and other materials to prevent the ground from drawing away your body heat. Most of our body heat is lost through ground transfer, so making the walls as dense as possible will ensure your protection.

There are many different types of survival shelters, and the design should fit the circumstances. Some shelters can be made from a plastic tarp, a rain poncho, cordage, and some rocks. You can also tie the tarp to a tree with more cordage. Using natural materials can make building a shelter easier. Just remember that you should only store enough food and water to last until your family can return to civilization.

One of the most important aspects to remember about survival is making sure you know where you are, or at least where your area of operation is. You must first assess your surroundings and properly map out your territory before starting any project that will prolong your life. Start by marking the sun's location from all positions from where you find yourself. You can determine specific directions by using sticks or naturally occurring features, such as a large tree with an exposed root system at its base. Mark your path throughout the day, and ensure that it is easily visible for future reference. This simple act will make finding your way home much easier.

Once you know where you are, it's important to realize what kind of weather conditions you'll be facing throughout the seasons. For most wilderness survival situations, three major factors influence survivability: temperature, precipitation, and wind speed. When constructing a shelter for yourself, these conditions must be considered as they can make or break your chances of making it out alive.

**Types of Outdoor Shelters**

Many forms of shelter can be constructed from whatever material may be available to you, including natural formations such as cliff overhangs and caves. In most cases, though, you will need to utilize your environment and build a shelter from materials found in the area. The most common forms of outdoor shelters are:

**Temporary Shelters**

These include any man-made structure that is constructed to provide immediate protection from the elements. While most people find themselves without a tent or any supplies during an emergency, they can still utilize what is around them to their advantage. Anything that will provide you with cover from both the sun and precipitation will suffice until a more suitable shelter can be constructed.

The key point to remember is that temporary shelters are your first line of defense against the environment. They are meant to be used until you have the proper tools and materials to build a more permanent shelter or until it's safe enough for you to move on. Temporary shelters do not require flooring nor even elaborate roofing. All that is truly needed are three walls and a simple roof. Any shaded spot where you can get away from the direct rays of the sun will suffice for a temporary shelter.

If there is no shaded area that can provide relief for your temporary shelter, it's important to be extremely careful when considering where you rest for the night. Even if it means crawling out of the sun, you must make sure that your area is free of any threat of wildlife or potential rainfall. Any moisture coming in contact with your skin can contribute to hypothermia, which will cut your survival time in half.

It's also important to realize that black and white are natural colors for camouflage when constructing a temporary shelter. Any dark colors will absorb the sun's rays, while lighter colors will reflect them. Use this to your advantage by always utilizing white or natural coloration whenever you can. You can do this by covering yourself with leaves or pine needles, laying on the natural soil around you, and placing rocks and sticks in specific patterns.

### A Lean-to Shelter

The lean-to is perhaps the best type of shelter to construct if you're stranded without a tent, especially during the spring and summer months when precipitation isn't as likely. To build one, it's important to find an abandoned tree with a substantial amount of leafy vegetation or use palm fronds in tropical climates.

Once you have found the perfect spot, large lean poles up against it at a forty-five-degree angle, leaving enough space between them for you to fit inside comfortably. For larger leaves, lay your poles parallel to one another so that they are facing opposite directions about four feet away from the tree, and then lay smaller poles on top of these to create your walls.

For the roof, stack branches on top of each other, creating a strong foundation for palm fronds or any vegetation with long stems. Once these have been placed evenly across the beams, cover them with leaves or large ferns, and then finally, the vegetation with long stems.

The lean-to should be covered in black or dark brown material to create a temporary shelter that will blend into its surroundings. If no material is available, carefully find five or six palm fronds or any similar leafy vegetation. Take these back to your lean-to and carefully spread them across the top in a triangular formation. Once this has been done, cover the top with leaves or large ferns, and then finally, vegetation with long stems.

### A Mid-Term Shelter

If you're stranded without a tent and have been forced to live in your shelter for days at a time, you must create a more permanent structure. This will allow you to get out of the elements and wait out any potential rainfall or snowstorm until you can be rescued.

Consider using tree boughs for a shelter that will provide protection from the elements while still allowing you to remain mobile. To build this type of shelter, find three or more long tree boughs, and place them against one another at a forty-five-degree angle without any form of bark. Then tie the tops together using vines to keep them in place. Once this has been done, create walls around your shelter by laying two large branches parallel to each other on opposite sides.

Don't forget that you will need a roof to protect yourself from the elements. Lay more branches across these parallel walls and tie them together so they remain secure. Then, create a foundation for your shelter by laying down thick branches and palm fronds, and cover this with protective vegetation such as ferns or large leaves.

## A Permanent Shelter

If your time stranded has been extended to several months, it may be time to build a more permanent shelter. To do this, find three thick poles around seven feet long, and pound them into the ground with a rock or similar heavy object. Then, attach these poles at the top using vines or lianas. Once these have been secured, build up walls using tree boughs in conjunction with any long, thick vegetation you can find.

Since the ground in your area may still be very wet from rainfall or snowfall, it's important to line the floor of your shelter with a waterproof material such as large leaves or palm fronds. Next, lay down small branches and ferns across the floor in a way that creates several spaces to accommodate you, your supplies, and any makeshift bedding. Once this has been done, create additional vegetation walls that separate each space into an area to sleep or store supplies.

Mapping out the area around your shelter will ensure you don't wake up surrounded by predators. It's important to note that certain creatures may want nothing to do with you, depending on the area of your operation. For instance, deer and other herbivores will usually not come near your shelter if you are in a forested area. It's also very beneficial to you to run along the perimeter of your shelter every morning to ensure that you are not being surrounded by any predators or other creatures who pose a threat to your safety.

A good rule of thumb is to slowly start walking outwards from where you sleep at night until you hear sounds of life, and then mark the perimeter. This way, you'll know where not to go during your runs so as not to disturb possible food sources. When deciding where to set up your shelter, also keep an eye out for dangerous obstacles such as large anthills or nests. If you find yourself near one of these, it's best to move away and relocate your camp so as not to anger the wildlife living there.

## Shelter Characteristics

The kind of shelter you need to build will be dependent on the weather you are dealing with and the resources you have. It is a good idea to familiarize yourself with the specifics of your situation thoroughly. In this section, I will cover as many different kinds of shelters as possible. You can then adapt these to suit your situation, what you have, and need. Various shelters you can build include:

## Lean-To

You have probably seen lean-to shelters plenty of times in movies and picture books, and they are an elementary kind of shelter that is easy to build with many different types of resources. A lean-to is usually used in areas with plenty of wood available, and it can provide shelter from rain, wind, snow, and cold. However, because the end is open, it isn't enormously warm.

Many people build a fire at the entrance to the lean-to to warm the inside and prevent heat from escaping from the shelter. Be careful if you will do this and make sure sparks cannot spread to your shelter.

Lean-to shelters are ideal because they are quick and easy to build. You can use any cliff face, large boulder, tree, or other structure to form the back wall of the lean-to and then lean wood up against it. This kind of shelter is flexible and can be made with almost anything, as long as you have access to poles. Lean-to shelters can be made warmer by insulating them and waterproofing the outside with moss, grass, or plastic.

## BUG OUT

### Platform Shelter

A platform shelter can be useful if you are in a situation where staying at ground level is unsafe; This may be because of animals or insects that could bite, sting, or otherwise attack you, especially when sleeping. A platform shelter is designed to get you off the ground and out of harm's way.

Platform shelters won't be possible to build in all situations, and they tend to require more skill. What you build will have to be able to support your weight reliably, or you might fall. You need to have practiced building one of these shelters in advance because otherwise, you are unlikely to be able to build it well enough to be secure. You are also very likely to need tools to build a platform shelter safely, which you may not have available.

However, there are situations in which you will need to make a platform shelter, and you may find you have the resources to do it, depending on your environment, so it's worth having this kind of shelter in your database.

### Snow Cave

If you are caught in snowy conditions, a snow cave is the easiest kind of shelter you can build, although you will need a suitable spade or shovel, or you will put yourself in danger of freezing when it takes to make one of these.

A snow cave is built into a snowdrift, and it is an excellent way to escape from the wind chill, hostile creatures, precipitation, and more. It will not be particularly warm, and it is possible to maintain the internal temperature at around 32 degrees F. This could keep you alive in freezing conditions. Your body heat will be crucial for keeping the cave warm.

### Leaf Hut

A leaf hut will provide you with a warm, reasonably large, enclosed area, and it is easy to build if you can find the right natural resources (wooden poles, leaves, etc.). Leaf huts can be warm and dry because of the insulating layer of leaves, and they are a great option if you are going to stay in one place for a while.

Leaf huts often take some time to build because they require a lot of materials, and they will be impossible in many areas (e.g., if you are somewhere with few trees), but they will work well in some situations.

Leaf huts can be adapted to suit ongoing needs and may be suitable for larger groups. They are also warmer than a lean-to shelter because they are mainly enclosed beside the door to keep heat loss to a minimum.

### Debris Shelter

A debris shelter is much simpler to make and requires fewer materials, although you will still need long poles to build one. There will be three poles necessary for this kind of shelter, and you'll need to gather up lots of leaf litter to cover the shelter with.

Debris shelters tend to be easy to create, but they can't be made in areas without leaves and strong sticks. You will require one of the poles to be taller than your head height.

### Tepee

You have probably seen tepees on TV and in books, and they are often associated with foreign countries. A tepee is one of the few shelters initially designed to hold fire, with a central hole to let smoke vent from inside. However, you should be very cautious about building a fire inside one of these despite the design; it could still be unsafe.

Traditionally, tepees were made using wooden poles and animal skins, and they were designed to be easily transportable. You can take them down and assemble them quickly, but they are not enormously easy to build in the wilderness, and if you don't have any experience in doing so, they may not be the best shelter. A tepee may be impractical unless you have easy access to tarpaulins and wooden poles. However, they do have their uses, and if you have the materials, they are one of the few shelters you can take with you when you travel.

## Ramada Shelter

A ramada shelter is used mainly for protection from the sun, as it has no walls; it is just an overhead shelter. It will not trap heat around you or reduce the wind or rain, but it will keep the sun off you. If you are in a hot area, this kind of shelter could be invaluable for survival.

Some ramada shelters do have one wall to increase the shade they provide, but most are open to improve air movement and keep the insides cool. If you want to include a wall, make sure you are not blocking the wind from entering the shelter because this will help keep the temperatures low. Ramada shelters can be made from anything readily available, but they often incorporate a piece of fabric as the main overhead part. Other materials tend to be in short supply in arid regions, so you may not have access to wood or other plant matter with which to weave a shade.

## Pit Shelter

A pit shelter can be ideal if you don't have a lot of materials, and it's an excellent way to hide if you don't want your shelter to be very obvious. This kind of shelter is usually semi-permanent because a lot of work goes into hollowing out the ground, and it won't be transportable. A pit shelter is a lot easier to make if you have a shovel, but it can be dug out by hand if necessary.

You still need natural resources to make the roof of a pit shelter. It will have a door for you to access the dugout through and should protect you from rain, sun, and other bad weather. Dugouts have some advantages: they are highly customizable, and it's easy to make storage space and seating arrangements. They are also an excellent way to get out of the wind almost entirely without building dense walls.

However, you may have issues with drainage, and it can be challenging to heat a pit shelter. If it rains a lot, you will need to make sure the water drains away from the parts of the pit shelter you use, or it will become impractical and uncomfortable.

It is sometimes safe to have a fire in a pit shelter, but you will need to make sure the shelter is extremely well ventilated to do this. If you are going to be stuck in the wild for a long time, a pit shelter is an excellent option.

## Igloo

Unlike a snow cave, an igloo is built of snow blocks rather than carved into a snowdrift. It lets you choose where to put the igloo, but it does mean a lot more work.

Igloos tend to be relatively large and may be an excellent way to shelter a large group if the conditions are bad. They take a lot of work to build, and you must know how to build one to ensure that the dome is stable, or it could be an unsafe shelter. Only practiced, skilled survivalists should attempt to build igloos, although they are probably the best option for long-term sheltering in the snow.

## Quinzhee

Quinzhees are like snow caves, but instead of simply using a snowdrift where you happen to find one, you will pile the snow up in a convenient area. It will then be hollowed out to create a cave, allowing you to get out of the wind.

It takes quite a long time and a lot of energy to make a quinzhee, so make sure you are up to the task. If you are already exhausted and cold, make a snow cave instead to have somewhere to retreat to, and think about building a more convenient shelter when you have rested and got warm.

## Fallen Tree Shelter

If you find a fallen tree, this can be an excellent option for making a shelter for yourself. Fallen trees will provide you with a ready-made structure that you can work with, saving you enormous amounts of time. However, you should make sure that the tree is stable before you start using it to build a shelter, or you could be risking your safety.

Fallen trees can be used to create lean-to shelters, but you can also drape a tarp or a blanket over one if you have these materials available. Peg the four corners out with stones, and you've got a makeshift shelter with very little time needed.

## A-Frame Shelter

An a-frame shelter is quick and easy to build and makes an excellent alternative to the lean-to if you cannot find a wall to build against. You will need a long, sturdy branch, plus shorter sticks, so this is best made in woodland. You can prop up both ends of the branch to make a level roof or just prop up one end and make a shelter that narrows to the ground at one end.

This shelter can be reasonably warm and cozy, although it shares the lean-to's disadvantage of having open ends that heat can escape through. A-frame shelters can be made in varying sizes to suit the number of people you need to shelter or make room for provisions/gear.

## How to Make a Shelter Safe

As you begin to build your shelter, ensure it is easily camouflaged with dirt or foliage from the area. In addition to this, elevate the shelter off the ground as much as possible. This will help avoid being submerged in floods, should they occur. If you're noticing that the weather has become wetter, it's time to move your camp before you are completely overcome by water or mud.

Thereafter, your shelter will need to include walls and roofing. If you can find sheets of fabric or large pieces of plastic in your supplies, they can be tied together with rope and used for this purpose. Otherwise, you can use vines or tree bark to lash together the necessary materials. If you can find a large enough stone, it can also be used as a wall.

You will begin to notice that bugs and small animals are attracted to your shelter, so you will need to position curtains or other walls, if possible, higher than the reach of these pests. If you do not have any additional vines or fabric, using your clothing is the next best thing. Even if you do, having a second layer of protection can help keep out crawling insects that might carry disease.

You'll also need to create a bed with insulation, which will help regulate your body temperature when it's too hot or too cold outside. If you have carpeting or towels with you, they can be used as

# PREPPER'S LONG-TERM SURVIVAL GUIDE

insulation and placed on the floor of your shelter. Otherwise, you can pile up leaves or fresh grass for this purpose.

If you plan on starting any fires, ensure your shelter is located a good distance away from the flame to avoid breathing in too much smoke. When you are ready to go to sleep at night, you should put out all of your fires for this reason as well. Although the fire may keep you warm, the smoke can irritate your throat and lungs and will prevent you from having a good night's rest.

If you're finding it difficult to find food and clean water because of where you are located, then it might be time for you to move on. You should only remain in one place if there is an abundant supply of food and water. If, however, you notice that the animals and insects are becoming scarce, it might be time to move on.

When it comes to shelter, as much as possible, plan what materials you will need and where you will go before disaster strikes. Keep a supply of good quality materials, such as rope and fabric, on hand to use in your shelter. In addition, ensure that you can find ample supplies of fresh water and food nearby before you settle down for the night. If possible, learn how to create your own tools and structures so that you do not have to rely on anyone else for assistance.

If you find yourself in a scenario where there is no possible way to call for rescue, you must know how to survive without any key tools or supplies. While this guide offers suggestions for surviving using materials found in nature, the best course of action is ensuring your shelter is equipped with everything you might need before you even begin to build.

A good example would be creating a hammock using hanging vines and two sturdy trees. This will keep you safe from the elements, allow you to store supplies in between your feet while sleeping, and provide protection in case of flooding or heavy rainfall. Although it may seem like extra work when there are more important things to do, always keep your shelter stocked with some of the supplies you are stranded with. If you find yourself in this situation, it means that rescue may not yet be on its way, and you must be equipped to survive by yourself for however long it takes.

A shelter will be necessary to keep you out of the sun, avoid the risk of heat stroke, and keep provisions fresh – but what other techniques can you employ?

Soak your clothes. You should only do this if you have water to spare, but it's a good way to cool off if you need to stay active when the weather is hot.

Wear long sleeves; This might sound counter-intuitive when you want to strip down as little as possible, but long sleeves will protect you from the sun. The same goes for long pants and a hat if possible — although not a woolly one.

Work in the coolest parts of the day, the morning and the evening. When the sun is at its hottest, retreat to your shelter and stay cool.

Prioritize staying hydrated because this allows you to sweat, keeping you cool. Make sure you have a good supply of water and the means to collect and purify more if you are in a hot area.

If your water is too limited to soak your clothes, but you can spare a little, wet a headscarf and tie it around your neck or wrists. The blood supply is close to the surface, so the cooling will be more effective.

Remember that the ground can be cool, so if you aren't in a desert, digging yourself a hollow in the shade may help you cool off. Mud can also protect you from the sun's heat and reduce the risk of sunburn.

# BUG OUT

Your emergency kit should contain one gallon of water per person per day. It's also important to note this water should be boiled and purified with tablets before drinking. In addition to your emergency food supply which will primarily consist of protein bars, you'll need a whistle, a knife or multi-tool, a flashlight or headlamp, a canteen, a radio with spare batteries, two pairs of socks, and one pair of gloves or mittens.

Be sure to include any necessary medications in your kit as well. While this is most important for those with health problems or allergies, if you've managed to cause an open wound while stranded, it's best to have antiseptic wipes on hand in case the injury begins to fester. You'll also need a map of the area, a compass, and a flare gun if you have one.

Whenever you're not using any supplies from your emergency kit, make sure they're kept dry and above ground level to ensure everything stays in good condition. Most importantly, be sure to drink plenty of water before going to sleep at night. If you're sweating during the day, collect fresh water to store for later.

## Communication Strategy

Maintain constant contact with the members of your emergency preparedness team. Save their phone numbers, write down their work and home addresses, and keep them informed of any potential dangers or changes in circumstances. It may be advantageous to hold a group discussion so that everyone in the group is aware of the situation without having to contact everyone individually. Don't overuse this mode of communication; if you message potential dangers too frequently, people may become desensitized to true S.H.T.F. circumstances.

In the aftermath of a disaster or during a survival party, incoming information is critical. Incoming information can be obtained from a variety of sources, such as Emergency Alert radios, NOAA weather radios, and over-the-air television. However, information input from these sources is only passive; they do not allow for interaction. As a result, it is critical to always have at least one radio with you. Here are some suggestions for improving your communication skills.

## The one-way radio

Many of you have a radio in your home, even if it's only the one in your vehicle or truck. I'll begin my tour of prepper communication alternatives with one-way radios, so-called because information only goes one way—to you from the transmitting channel or station.

## AM/FM

For decades, AM/FM radio has already been ubiquitous, and it is the first element that jumps to mind whenever the subject of radio is mentioned. Despite recent technological breakthroughs, there is much to be said for plain, old-fashioned broadcast radio.

What makes this noteworthy? Local news stations may be unable to transmit if the tragedy is regional. However, stations outside the impacted region will undoubtedly share whatever information they can acquire, and it is through them that you may discover more of what's going on.

## Satellite Radio

Satellite radio has grown in popularity over the previous several years. It is a subscription service, and you must have satellite radio to hear the broadcasts. The pure enjoyment value of satellite radio is unrivaled. I spend plenty of time driving my vehicle and have learned to appreciate the variety of alternatives provided by my Sirius membership.

The majority of the channels specialize in a single genre, like old-time radio broadcasts, 1980s hair metal, and Jimmy Warren buffet beach music. Naturally, there are news channels of different kinds, such as CNN.

## Shortwave

Shortwave (SW) communications may be transmitted across the globe by reflecting them off the ionosphere, which is called for the high ion concentration in this layer of the atmosphere, which is located 50 to 600 miles above the Earth's surface. You may listen to transmissions from all across the world in this iron-rich atmosphere. SW radio, unlike amateurs (HAM) radio, is just one way. A station sends out a signal, and you receive it. You can't converse back on an SW radio.

## Two-way radio

## Telephones

Everyone reading this guide is probably familiar with telephones. Even if you're one of the few people who doesn't keep a phone in their pocket, I'm sure you've seen them before. When it comes down to it, I'm sure you'd figure it out. As a result, I won't be spending much time using telephones as a mode of communication. However, there are a few points to consider.

Cell towers may quickly become overburdened in an emergency. While you may have a strong signal when using your phone, calls will not be answered due to the high volume of calls. This has happened several times during major disasters. Text messages, on the other hand, are frequently delivered. This is due to the way networks are constructed. If you can't reach your relatives by phone, try texting them and see if that helps.

## FRS/GMRS

The idea was to set aside a block of frequencies that would not require a test, licensing application, or additional red tape to operate. Allowing a customer to buy a set of two-way communicators and use them to communicate with family and friends, such as while attending special events.

## MURS

MURS frequencies are used less frequently than GMRS or FRS frequencies. However, I believe this is more due to ignorance than anything else. The FCC designated five frequencies previously used only by businesses as license-free and open to the public in 2000.

MURS radios are typically portable, but larger, permanent base unit versions are also available. The handhelds typically have a range of about 2 kilometers, depending on topography. The base units are connected to larger external antennas, allowing for ranges of up to 10 miles.

## Walkie-talkies

Walkie-talkies are an essential survival tool, even if you don't realize it. In a disaster or other emergency situation, they provide critical communication. While walkie-talkies aren't the best communication devices, they are useful for a variety of other purposes. Some of the ways walkie-talkies can help you during a disaster are listed below. You can also use them for fun activities like camping with your family. You can also use them on a construction site. Even in this day and age of mobile phones, walkie-talkies remain extremely useful.

## BUG OUT

The first consideration is the range of the walkie-talkies. In an emergency where you don't have access to a phone signal, you'll need them to communicate. This is due to the fact that walkie-talkies are not dependent on cell phone signals. They can communicate over distances of up to 12 kilometers because they use radio signals. They can also connect to over eight channels, allowing you to communicate without touching the device.

Consider the battery life and range when purchasing walkie-talkies for survival preps. In an emergency, cell towers and phone lines may be down, so walkie-talkies are the only way for people to communicate. These two-way radios are ideal for a small group or family. They'll also come in handy for group communication in a survival situation where you need to communicate with others in a remote location.

A basic walkie-talkie is ideal if you don't have a lot of money to spend on them. It is water-resistant and has a few channels. It has a five-mile range, making it an excellent backup set. If you intend to use your walkie-talkies for vehicle travel, look for long-range walkie-talkies. This device operates on GMR (General Mobile Radio Service) frequencies and provides a strong signal.

A walkie-range talkie for survival prepping varies greatly. If the device is used in the wild, the range should be between two and five miles. The communication distance is determined by the device used. An FRS set, for example, may only have a few miles of range. The greater the range, the more effective the communication. When you're out in the wilderness, this is crucial.

### CB radios

If you're looking for a good CB radio for survival prepping, there are several models to choose from. The Standard Horizon model, for example, has many features, including an illuminated screen, a multi-function LCD screen, and a roger beep. These radios also come with an auxiliary power source and an adapter to connect to an external speaker. And if you want to be able to play music from your smartphone, there's a CB radio that has those features, as well.

If you need a CB radio that fits in a backpack or other small space, President Bill, a compact survival radio about the size of a mobile phone, is highly recommended. It has noise-canceling filters and auto squelch system. It also has a USB charging port for other devices and a loudspeaker, allowing you to communicate even during thunderstorms.

Keep in mind that CB radios are more portable than most. A portable CB radio takes up the least amount of room and can easily fit into a bug-out bag. They are also frequently powered by batteries or a cigarette lighter adapter, making them ideal for communicating while away from a location. Some models include a basic antenna, such as a rubber ducky, which provides adequate results but may require upgrading in the future.

When selecting a CB radio for survival prep, keep in mind that not every CB radio has all of the features you'll require. CB radios can be used by multiple people, but you must choose one with specific channels. If you're using a CB radio for emergencies, use channel nine, while channel nineteen is reserved for truckers and other emergency communications.

A CB radio can help you stay in touch with family and friends if you're bugging in as a prepper. When SHTF, having a means of communication will be critical. It will not only save your life, but it will also be a lot of fun! Don't forget to look through Amazon UK's entire selection of CB radios. You'll be glad you have one for your SHTF planning!

### Morse code

The use of the Morse Code for survival prepping is becoming more popular, but how can you really benefit from this type of communication? Not only can it be an essential tool in a survival situation, but it can also serve a practical purpose like sending messages or dirty jokes. Listed below are some practical applications for Morse Code, and how you can use it in your prepping arsenal. To learn more, read on!

First, you may already be aware of the value of learning how to use Morse Code. During emergencies, you can use this code to communicate with others in distress. You'll be able to relay information using Morse messages more efficiently and accurately than by using voice communication. And even if you don't need to call on a ham radio for communication, you can use flashlights or other types of devices to send messages. Another practical survival prepping use for Morse Code is in case of a natural disaster.

Once you know the basics of Morse Code, you can begin practicing with the use of a flashcard app. These apps are similar to educational programs, but they display random letters and numbers. Some of them will even allow you to practice translating sentences! If you're a parent, it's a good idea to find a flashcard app that teaches this skill. It's easy to get a free trial and try it out! You'll be happy you did!

Another useful survival prep tool is a high-quality, high-decibel survival whistle. It is one of the most effective SOS signals around and can mean the difference between a survivalist and an improvised rescue squad. During the dark, flashlights can also be used as Morse code signals. A high-lumen flashlight can help you send out messages through the night. This method is simple and can be interpreted by anyone.

### Sign language

When a disaster strikes, it is crucial to have multiple ways of communicating. While you can use sign language alphabets, you can also learn to read lips. This can come in handy during emergency situations when normal communication is severely compromised. Sign language is a powerful tool for survival preppers. You can learn it in less than 5 minutes using a free ASL video. You can also create secret signals for emergencies to communicate with others.

### Land Navigation Techniques

Whether you know where you are going or happen to find yourself lost, being able to read a map and use a compass are vital outdoor survival skills. Here are some tips for navigation in the wilderness.

Learn how to read a map effectively. Although it is more difficult to read, a Military Grid Reference System map is preferable to a latitude-longitude map. It will take some time and practice, but it will be worthwhile.

Along with knowing how to read a map, you should also know how to use a compass. On the market, there are various types of compasses.

> **Button compass:** Commonly found in automobiles, this type of compass is useful for simply getting your bearings and determining direction. If you don't know where you are or which direction to go, it's difficult to navigate through the woods.

***Mountaineering compass (orienteering compass):*** A magnetic needle points in the direction of the magnetic north. It has a direction dial that rotates, median lines that can be oriented according to longitudinal lines on a map, and a travel direction arrow.

***Lensmatic and prismatic compasses:*** These are orienteering compasses with additional features like glow-in-the-dark directional arrows and phosphorous features.

The difference between magnetic north and true north is referred to as declination. Declination changes annually and can vary from the eastern to the western side of a country. You will need to regularly adjust the declination on your compass.

## Common Compass Errors

- Metal objects such as bushcraft tools, zippers, and even your watch can interfere with your compass.
- Using your compass instead of a map to determine your travel direction.
- Holding the compass incorrectly.
- Keeping your gaze fixed on your compass rather than using visual bearing indicators such as landmarks.
- Checking your bearing on a regular basis.
- Failure to adjust your compass for declination. Failure to learn how to read and use a compass properly.
- It is not as easy as using a GPS. These navigation options, on the other hand, will get you from where you are to where you want to go.
- It only takes a little practice to truly understand this, so you could begin studying as soon as today.

Natural navigational techniques can be lost if you don't have a map or compass with you or lose them while in the wilderness. All of these techniques require you to be intimately familiar with the area you'll be in so you know what to look for and what to use as navigational cues. Have a map handy when learning these techniques so you can follow the instructions visually.

Handrails are things like trails, roads, pipelines, creeks, and so on that, you can use to get to your destination. They can also serve as stoppers.

Backstops are frequently handrails that alert you when you've strayed too far in one direction and need to change your path.

Baselines are used to help you get back to where you started. They could be creeks, roads, or trails, for example. The only requirements are that they run past your point, are easily visible so that you don't cross them by accident, are relatively straight, and are of significant length. Assume your starting point is located along a generally north-south roadway and you depart from your camp in a north-easterly direction. You arrive at your destination, but it's not always as simple as turning around and returning. You could easily deviate from your original path of travel or go in circles. Determine whether you want to travel south-southwesterly or north-northwesterly from your destination. If you were traveling north-east from your camp, you will be in a south-westerly direction when you turn around. Traveling more north or south of south-west will put you almost exactly where you want to be on your baseline. If you choose to travel north-northwest, turn left when you reach your baseline to reach your camp. If you choose to travel south-southwest, turn right when you reach your baseline.

Aiming off means choosing a direction to travel in from your starting point and using baselines and handrails to help you along the way. This will assist you in reaching your destination and returning to your starting point. Let's pretend that your starting point is on a north-south highway. Your destination is located to the north-east. A combination handrail can be found to the north of your starting point. Assume your handrail is a path on a trail. To the east of that trail, there should be another handrail that connects to the path, such as a pipeline, and leads to your destination. If you go too far north and hit the trail, you can turn east and follow the trail to the pipeline junction. You know to turn south at the junction and follow the pipeline to your destination. The second handrail you must identify must intersect with your baseline and will assist you in returning to it. Assume that this handrail is a creek that runs east-west. When you leave your destination to return to your starting point, you will know to head south-west. You know to turn west and follow the creek back to your roadway baseline if you stray too far south of your starting point. Because you traveled south to your starting point, you will know to turn north when you reach the roadway, which will take you back to your starting point.

Blazing refers to marking a natural feature at or near your starting point on a baseline so that when you use the other four techniques to navigate, that marking will indicate that you have come back to your starting point.

As you can see, the first four techniques require you to intimately familiarize yourself with the area and terrain before you even leave home. That way, if you forget or lose your map, you can still make your way to a destination and back to your starting point again.

## Maps

You may have figured it out by now, but maps are your go-to item. While they are ineffective without a map to assist you in correcting your route and locating your location, they provide some geographical knowledge.

I'm not talking about GPS or smartphone maps here; I'm talking about paper maps. A localized map of your dwelling area or the region you want to bug out in will be helpful for navigation.

A map illustrates varied heights and routes and allows you to prepare properly for challenging places of travel for novice preppers or those who've never had to explore the country before.

## Compasses

Compasses may be used on their own, but they are best used in conjunction with maps. A compass shows cardinal directions in 360° increments. North is 0 degrees, East is 90 degrees, South is 180 degrees, & West is 270 degrees.

These are shown on the compasses rose, which is a plate that lies directly behind the needle and indicates which side is which. Otherwise, you'd only be able to locate the northern tip. For inexperienced navigators, this is insufficient to correctly carve a route.

You should use one of two kinds of compasses: a magnetic compass that always faces north, and a lensatic compass, which is used with maps to assist you in navigating over particular locations with great precision.

Finding North Without a Compass

If you don't have a compass and can't accurately tell which way is east and which is west by simply looking at the sun, you can use a shadow cast by the sun to help you find your bearings. If you are trying to navigate at night, you can use the moon and stars to help you find your way.

## Shadow Stick Method

- Using a shadow stick necessitates using the middle of the day.
- In a clearing, insert a long stick into the ground.
- Make a mark where the shadow's tip falls.
- Make several more marks as the sun reaches and then passes through its highest point at midday. After making several marks and the sun has passed the midday mark, use the shortest shadow to indicate north. If the moon is bright enough, this method can be used for nighttime navigation. Use the stick's shadow, taking advantage of the moon's shortest shadow when it is at its highest point in the sky.

## Making Use of the Stars

To navigate using the stars, you must be able to identify two constellations: the Big Dipper and the Little Dipper. Each dipper consists of two parts: a bowl and a handle.

Draw an imaginary line between the last star in the bowl of the Big Dipper and the last star in the handle of the Little Dipper, also known as the North Star. Polaris is the line that runs north from the Big Dipper to the Little Dipper.

## When You're Stuck

It's critical to know what steps to take if you're lost in the wilderness or suspect you're lost.

Admit that you have no idea where you are. Denial and continuing to blunder will only get you further lost.

Keep your cool. Your judgment is clouded by fear. Consider your movements, whether straight or turning, and the direction you were moving in.

# PREPPER'S LONG-TERM SURVIVAL GUIDE

Be observant and look for clues such as which way north is, footprints and the direction they are going, and visible and recognizable landmarks. Place a brightly colored waypoint marker somewhere high up. As long as you can see the marker and return to it, you can walk in any direction to try to find a familiar area or path.

- Use a GPS or phone to find your location if you have one. If you're fighting for a signal, use a waypoint marker to move around to find one.
- Stay in the area where you got lost; staying close to where you went off track makes it easier for help to find you. Within sight of a waypoint marker, build a shelter, find water, and find food. If necessary, find a higher vantage point with a view of a road, town, building, or recognizable landmark to help you orient yourself.
- Look for human signs and listen for footsteps or voices.
- Find an open area and prepare a signaling method to make yourself visible to rescue planes. Stay put when the sun goes down. Stumbling around at night is dangerous because it can lead to you going in circles because you can't see any signs of people or landmarks.

## Navigation Through the Heavens

Celestial navigation is the use of heavenly objects in the sky to determine where you have been, where you need to go, and how you will get there. While this type of navigation was not widely used commercially until the 1980s, the United States continues to rely on it for its accuracy.

For accurate celestial navigation, a sextant, a revolving instrument that determines your relative position to a celestial body, would be used.

By measuring your position against the curve of the earth, you can obtain a generalized region to visit. You can hone your celestial navigation skills over time to reach specific locations with pinpoint accuracy.

What should you do if you don't have all of the above items?

Even if you don't have any tools, you can explore. It isn't as simple as using the Hubble Space Telescope, but it is possible. Celestial navigation requires you to learn eight stars or constellations, which correspond to the eight points on a compass.

- The north star is Polaris.
- The Big Dipper is a star constellation that points to Polaris.
- Cassiopeia, but opposite the Big Dipper at the other end of Polaris.
- The Charioteer is a constellation that aids in locating Polaris.
- Polaris is reached via the Pegasus constellation.
- The Northern Cross also indicates Polaris.
- The Belt of Orion is another name for the Orion Constellation. The main star will always rise in the morning and set in the west, no matter where you are on the planet.
- Scorpius is the sign that always points south.
- Polaris, in case you haven't noticed, is extremely important. Polaris, the Orion Cluster, and Scorpius are important because they show you where the true north, west, south, and west are.

# BOOK 10: THE MOST FREQUENT SHTF SITUATIONS: TIPS AND TRICKS

# PREPPER'S LONG-TERM SURVIVAL GUIDE
# THE MOST FREQUENT SHTF SITUATIONS: TIPS AND TRICKS

**Bug Out Situations That Are Most Likely to Occur**

The following is a comprehensive list of several instances in which bugging out may be the most prudent course of action. Of course, every circumstance is unique, and only you can make the ultimate decision on whether or not you should remain in the position. These instances, on the other hand, may assist in making things more obvious.

Natural calamities are unavoidable. Wildfires, floods, and other devastating natural forces are all typical reasons for people to prepare for an emergency. Prepare for natural catastrophes in your region by being aware of their possibilities, having an evacuation plan in place, keeping your BOB close by, and listening to emergency broadcasts for weather alerts and evacuation orders. Stay informed about catastrophes impacting your neighborhood by signing up for an emergency alert service such as Nixle.

### Earthquakes

Earthquakes occur when the earth's tectonic plates collide and move in opposite directions. These plates occasionally move away from one another, but most of the time, they slide over or under one another. The rupturing of rock caused by this movement produces vibrations that we perceive as earthquakes. Tsunamis and volcanic eruptions can occur if the movements are massive. Plan to act quickly in the event of an earthquake.

- Place yourself beneath a sturdy table or against an interior wall.
- Keep windows, mirrors, hanging objects, and tall furniture out of the way.
- If you're outside, get out there and stay there. Check that there are no buildings nearby that could collapse on you.
- If you are in a vehicle, pull over in a safe location and remain in the vehicle. If there are no buildings nearby, exit and stay away from power lines.
- Prepare for a tsunami, landslide, or avalanche if there is an earthquake.

### Hurricanes

These are storms that form over tropical seas. They are accompanied by extremely strong winds and thunderstorms, which have catastrophic consequences for anything in their path. Hurricanes are one of the worst natural disasters you can encounter because they can destroy your home, ruin your property, and injure or even kill you. Hurricanes and tornadoes that form over land are the same thing. They are violent storms that function similarly to a vacuum cleaner. The winds that encircle them suck up everything in their path, wreaking havoc along the way.

If you live in a hurricane-prone area, take the necessary precautions by installing steel bars on your doors and windows.

Stay away from buildings and power lines if you're driving during a hurricane. If there is no other shelter nearby and you believe your car will be swept away, get out quickly and climb on top of it. You must not stand under a tree because, even if your car is not in danger, the tree may become uprooted and strike the vehicle or you.

Avoid rivers that flow into the ocean as well. Even if you're in a boat, you shouldn't get too close to them because an incoming tidal wave could sweep you up and drag you out to sea.

## SHTF SITUATION

### Volcanic Eruptions

During a volcanic eruption, you should do whatever you can to get away from it immediately because the heat coming from the volcano's mouth is extremely hot and could cause burns on your skin. If you're near or inside a building close to the volcano, get out of it. The roof and the walls might collapse from the weight of hot ash.

Keep an eye on the volcano's activity if you live in an area prone to volcanic eruptions. You can do this by contacting the volcanology and meteorology services to determine whether the volcano is active or dormant.

If the volcano is active and there are signs of an eruption, get out of your house as soon as possible because lava could start flowing from its mouth at any time. Make your way to higher ground, where you will be safe from landslides and tsunamis.

Avoid driving near bridges and power lines during a volcanic eruption because the ash released by the volcano may cause them to collapse. Do not attempt to cross rivers near where lava is flowing because their banks may be eroded by the intensity of the heat coming from the volcano.

If you smell or feel hot ash coming your way, cover your face with a cloth to avoid being burned. Avoid anything that could fall on you because even small pieces of rock can cause serious injuries if they land on you.

### Lightning

Lightning is extremely dangerous because it is not only extremely hot when it strikes but also composed of highly charged particles that can pass through your skin and into your muscles. If you are caught in a lightning storm and there is no shelter nearby, crouch into a ball with your hands on top of your head and avoid flinching or jerking because you must not lose your balance and fall over whatever happens. If lightning strikes above you, you'll be hit if you're standing up straight.

When a storm is approaching, keep an eye on your surroundings because heavy rain means there's a good chance it'll turn into a thunderstorm.

If you live in a lightning-prone area, stay away from tall buildings because they can attract lightning strikes. Avoid anything metal, such as doors, windows, and so on.

When a storm is approaching, never lie flat on the ground because lightning can strike you from the surface of the water.

If you're in a vehicle and it enters a storm, pull over immediately because your vehicle may attract lightning strikes if its metal parts conduct electricity. Don't go under trees, either, because they attract lightning as well.

If you're driving and a thunderstorm begins, don't reach out the window to wipe raindrops off the car because you could come into direct contact with the lightning.

Make sure your car's electrical system is properly grounded so that if lightning strikes nearby, it does not pass through the vehicle and electrocute you.

If there is a chance of lightning, never stand in a puddle of water because it can cause serious injuries or even death if struck by lightning.

### Wildfires

Wildfires are caused by a variety of factors, including lightning strikes and vehicle sparks. They have the ability to burn down entire farms and homes as well as trees. They are extremely dangerous because they can spread at lightning speeds and cause enough damage to destroy vital items. A wildfire can be extremely dangerous because it can burn your skin and ignite anything it comes into contact with. The best thing you can do during a wildfire is to stay away from it and, if possible, seek shelter in buildings.

Keep an eye on the movement of the wildfire by checking online or with news channels, weather reports, and so on.

When you detect a wildfire nearby, avoid anything flammable, such as trees, shrubs, and wood furniture, which can quickly catch fire.

Keep hydrated because wildfires absorb all the water around them, making it difficult to drink anything that isn't bottled or boiled.

If you are in your car during a wildfire, continue driving until you find a safe place to park and stay in your car until the fire has been extinguished or is no longer a threat to you.

When a wildfire is nearby, keep the windows closed because gusts of air from outside can fan the flames and blow them inside your home. Keep everyone together so that an adult can take charge if something goes wrong.

Never run through a wildfire because the intense heat and flames can cause your clothes to ignite, causing you to burst into flames and be burned alive. If escape is not possible, stay low to the ground and wrap yourself in thick blankets or other types of fireproof materials to protect yourself from the flames.

If you live in a wildfire-prone area, make sure your home is fireproof on the inside so that if a wildfire occurs, your family and home will be safe from the flames.

Keep an eye out for smoldering fires if you live in a wildfire zone because they can quickly spread if they ignite a nearby patch of grass. This is why wildfires are so difficult to put out once they've been started by something like lightning.

If you suspect a wildfire is approaching your home, make sure your lawn isn't dry because if the fire reaches it while you're away, it will spread to your home and destroy everything inside. To avoid this problem, have someone check it on a regular basis for dry conditions.

**Mudslides and floods**

Flooding and mudslides are common during heavy rains. They're especially dangerous because they can cause the ground to become extremely slippery and difficult to navigate, even in areas that appear to be flat enough. Floods and mudslides can also conceal manholes and other hazards that could result in serious injuries if you slip and fall into one.

Keep your car windows closed during a flood because water will quickly rise outside and begin to enter through them. Maintain an elevated position so that if your car is swept away, it does not crush you and cause serious injuries.

During a flood, stay safe and away from trees and power lines because they can be knocked over by strong winds and snap, falling on you.

When walking outside during a flood, keep an eye out for fallen branches that could knock you down and severely injure you.

# SHTF SITUATION

If you live in an area prone to flooding or mudslides, keep valuables away from downstairs areas because you don't want everything to be damaged if the ground becomes saturated with water and begins to collapse.

Always pay attention to weather reports when a flood is approaching your area because if a buildup of water is expected, they will always warn you ahead of time so that you can prepare.

## Infections and Diseases

In areas where there is a lot of pollution, trash, and bacteria in the ground, diseases and infections are very common. Some diseases are transmitted by mosquitos and other insects and animals, which carry them on/in their bodies before infecting you when bitten. The Covid virus has been reported to be transmitted in a similar manner, and it can cause severe bleeding without any visible signs of infection.

If someone in your vicinity begins vomiting or bleeding from their eyes or mouth, keep everyone away from them because they will infect anyone who comes into contact with them.

If you suspect someone in your vicinity has the Covid virus, keep your distance to prevent them from spreading it to you. If someone has it, they will constantly cough, complain of body aches, and lose their sense of taste or smell.

Keep your home clean at all times by discarding old food and drink containers, and wash your hands frequently because many diseases begin with an open wound or are spread through contact.

If you notice any unusual people around you who haven't cleaned themselves in several days, keep an eye on them because they may have contracted a disease that causes them to behave in this manner. It is best to report them to your local authorities as soon as possible so that they can deal with them.

## Food and Water Contamination

Food and water contamination is a serious problem because if you eat or drink something that's contaminated, it will begin to destroy your body from the inside and cause very painful illnesses over time. Other diseases like gastroenteritis and typhoid fever are also very common if you eat the wrong thing, so always be aware of where your food and water come from.

If you're in an area that's prone to contamination, keep track of any unusual or sickly-looking people around because they could have contaminated something that you might eat or drink.

If you think your food or water has been contaminated, throw it away immediately so that no one else gets sick after taking a bite or sip.

If you have to eat outside because of a disaster, know where your food comes from before you buy anything. Make sure that there isn't a sick or unusual-looking person who's been in contact with it because they could have made it unsafe for you to eat.

## Avalanches and Snowstorms

Avalanches and snowstorms are common, particularly during the cold winter months. They can result in massive casualties if people are not cautious when walking outside or driving their cars. The weight of the snow can become too much for you to bear, and it will eventually crush anything beneath the snow if there are no trees or rocks nearby to stop it.

- If you are outside during an avalanche or blizzard, never attempt to move or drive a car because you will be unable to see anything through the snow.

# PREPPER'S LONG-TERM SURVIVAL GUIDE

- If you're walking outside and get crushed by snow, use your hands to shovel away as much as you can as quickly as you can.
- If someone nearby is screaming for help because they are being crushed, start digging through the snow with your hands right away so you can save them before it's too late.
- If you know exactly where someone is buried beneath the snow, start digging in that exact spot so you can recover them before they suffocate under the snow.

Natural disasters can be avoided if you are aware of what is going on in your area and plan accordingly. Keep an eye out for any unusual people in your vicinity who may have come into contact with contaminated food or water, as they may be carrying a contagious illness that could make others sick. If you must be outside, always bring a first aid kit because it could save your life if something goes wrong. When you have a plan, surviving floods, earthquakes, and other natural disasters is much easier, so always be ready for anything that may occur in your area.

### Cyberspace Difficulties

Not long ago, cyber-attacks were thought to be absurd. Cyberterrorism, on the other hand, is now a serious threat. Hackers may disrupt the power grid, damage equipment, and even disable nuclear power plant safeguards. Identity theft and scams are also common occurrences. The world as we know it could end at the whim of an enraged programmer. When cybercriminals come knocking, go offline and hide somewhere where their electronic tentacles can't reach you.

### War

When conflict strikes close to home, civilians are only innocent victims of a ferocious conflict. As a result, you must defend yourself and seek safer grounds. Safety is a relative concept in nuclear warfare. Nuclear fallout will be a major issue, and any survivors from the first wave will barely survive. You'll have a much better chance of survival if you can get away before or shortly after the bombs go off.

Lastly, if looting, rioting and passive resistance are becoming more common in your neighborhood, it is important to go before the situation degenerates. Learn how to protect yourself as you flee to more stable grounds if you find yourself in an unexpected revolt.

# CONCLUSION

Thank you for reading this book. Natural disasters cannot be avoided. The majority of them are natural, but some, like war, are man-made. People cannot prevent a disaster from occurring. People must, however, learn to be prepared to deal with natural disasters and to stay alive in the event of a natural disaster.

The world we now inhabit is unpredictable and dangerous. We never know when something will happen that will make it impossible for us to leave our homes or find the items we require on a daily basis, such as food, home defense, first aid, and so on. On the other hand, this guide provides you with all the information you need to stay safe in an emergency.

It is a wise decision to plan ahead of time. It is not only important to be prepared for the worst; it is also important to be prepared to survive and thrive in any situation. This book is useful for anyone who is not a prepper or a survivalist. This guide has something for everyone, whether you want to learn more about prepping or how to prepare for common emergencies.

It's easy to become overwhelmed when it comes to being a prepper. You can, however, survive anything the world throws at you with time, patience, and understanding.

The first step is to prepare your home for the disaster. Hopefully, this book has shown you the value of being prepared for a disaster or emergency. While it is hoped that you will never be forced to use these supplies, it is always a good idea to be prepared. So, take the time to read this book and be well-equipped and prepared for whatever comes your way.

Worse, most people who are affected by disasters are unprepared. In other cases, they are unsure of how to respond effectively in an emergency. The good news is that you have access to this comprehensive beginner's guide to risk preparation and management. We created this useful workbook with people like you in mind.

If you lack the necessary skills to deal with these issues, you may find yourself in a dangerous or even life-threatening situation. This book has covered a variety of topics that you should be aware of when dealing with a crisis.

Rescue and survival skills for each type of disaster can save your life. When you read this survival workbook, you will realize that saving your life and the lives of your loved ones is not that difficult. This handbook is unique in that it has been meticulously compiled to include all of the details about emergencies that you should be aware of. The good news is that it is possible to plan for various types of emergencies. This is the essence of this book: to assist you and your loved ones in overcoming such difficulties.

Good luck.

# PREPPER'S LONG-TERM SURVIVAL GUIDE

## REFERENCES

Everett, W. (2019, August 15). Getting started with selfsufficient living (and why it IS possible). Insteading.Com. https://insteading.com/blog/selfsufficient-living/

Ishak, R. (2016, March 28). 6 ways to be more selfsufficient. Bustle.Com; Bustle. https://www.bustle.com/articles/147230-6-ways-to-be-more-selfsufficient-independent McCoy, D. (2019, August 8). 41 ways to become more selfsufficient • the rustic elk. Therusticelk.Com. https://www.therusticelk.com/41-ways-to-become-more-self-sufficient/

Poindexter, J. (2017, March 9). What selfsufficient living is about and 8 tips on how to achieve it. Morningchores.Com. https://morningchores.com/selfsufficient-living/

Rakes, M. (2015, January 12). 18 Easy Ways to Become More SelfSufficient. Gracefullittlehoneybee.Com. https://www.gracefullittlehoneybee.com/18-easy-ways-become-selfsufficient/

Survivalists reveal genius tips for selfsufficient living. (n.d.). Loveproperty.Com. Retrieved from https://www.loveproperty.com/gallerylist/95567/survivalists-reveal-genius-tips-for-selfsufficient-living Mayntz, M. (n.d.). SelfSufficient Living Tips. Lovetoknow.Com; LoveToKnow Media. Retrieved from https://greenliving.lovetoknow.com/Self_Sufficient_Living_Tips

Selfsufficiency. (2015, June 17). Econation.Co.Nz. https://www.econation.co.nz/selfsufficiency/

Nester, T. (2013). When the Grid Goes Down: Disaster Preparations and Survival Gear For Making Your Home Self-Reliant Paperback – January 9, 2013. Diamond Creek Publishing.

The Prepper. (n.d.). Retrieved from The Prepper website: https://theprepared.com/

Snyder, M. (n.d.). The Economic Collapse Blog. The Economic Collapse Blog website: http://theeconomiccollapseblog.com

Selfsufficiency: An essential aspect of well-being. (n.d.). Psychology Today. Retrieved from https://www.psychologytoday.com/us/blog/out-the-darkness/201303/selfsufficiency-essential-aspect-well-being The importance of self-reliance. (2020, July 20). Theguesthouseocala.Com. https://www.theguesthouseocala.com/the-importance-of-self-reliance/

van den Toren, S. J., van Grieken, A., de Kroon, M. L. A., Mulder, W. C., Vanneste, Y. T. M., & Raat, H. (2020). Young adults' selfsufficiency in daily life: the relationship with contextual factors and health indicators. BMC Psychology, 8(1), 89.

What is Self-Reliance and How to Develop It? (2019, April 15). Positivepsychology.Com. https://positivepsychology.com/self-reliance/

Why It's Important to Be SelfSufficient (+ How it Can Help you Save). (2016, April 10). Thecentsableshoppin.Com. https://www.thecentsableshoppin.com/why-its-important-to-be-self-sufficient-how-it-can-help-you-save/

Austin, H. B. (2016, April 10). The issues with selfsufficiency. Psu.Edu. https://sites.psu.edu/futureoffood/2016/04/10/the-issues-with-self-sufficiency/

Ramsey, C. (2020, February 3). Overcoming the challenges of a selfsufficiency approach. Barnett-Waddingham.Co.Uk; Barnett Waddingham. https://www.barnett-waddingham.co.uk/comment-insight/blog/over-coming-the-challenges-of-a-selfsufficiency-approach/

Selfsufficiency: An essential aspect of well-being. (n.d.). Psychology Today. Retrieved from https://www.psychologytoday.com/us/blog/out-the-darkness/201303/selfsufficiency-essential-aspect-well-being van den Toren, S. J., van Grieken, A., de Kroon, M. L. A., Mulder, W. C., Vanneste, Y. T. M., & Raat, H. (2020). Young adults' selfsufficiency in daily life: the relationship with contextual factors and health indicators. BMC Psychology, 8(1), 89.

What is Self-Reliance and How to Develop It? (2019, April 15). Positivepsychology.Com. https://positivepsychology.com/self-reliance/

(N.d.). Uwo.Ca. Retrieved from http://www.uwo.ca/fhs/nursing/WHES/files/Barriers%20Nov.pdf

Everett, W. (2019, August 15). Getting started with selfsufficient living (and why it IS possible). Insteading.Com. https://insteading.com/blog/selfsufficient-living/

Ishak, R. (2016, March 28). 6 ways to be more selfsufficient. Bustle.Com; Bustle. https://www.bustle.com/articles/147230-6-ways-to-be-more-selfsufficient-independent McCoy, D. (2019, August 8). 41 ways to become more selfsufficient • the rustic elk. Therusticelk.Com. https://www.therusticelk.com/41-ways-to-become-more-self-sufficient/

Poindexter, J. (2017, March 9). What selfsufficient living is about and 8 tips on how to achieve it. Morningchores.Com. https://morningchores.com/selfsufficient-living/

Rakes, M. (2015, January 12). 18 Easy Ways to Become More SelfSufficient. Gracefullittlehoneybee.Com. https://www.gracefullittlehoneybee.com/18-easy-ways-become-selfsufficient/

Stephanie, William, Dottie, & Farmer's Wife. (2017, February 20). 50 ways to become more selfsufficient in 1 hour or less. Therealfarmhouse.Com. http://www.therealfarmhouse.com/50-ways-to-become-more-self-sufficient-in-1-hour-or-less/

Printed in Great Britain
by Amazon